WHAT PEOPLE ARE SAYING ABOUT
COACH CHUCK DALY:

"Chuck did much more than co_____ vely impacted everyone he met, both person_____ ove of people and the game of basketball h_____ ____up the next generation of coaches."
— David Stern, NBA Commissioner

"Chuck was always a friend of coaches. A good guy. He was always in the coaching fraternity and always extended a friendly hand."
— Phil Jackson, Los Angeles Lakers head coach

"Chuck had a genuine humility that allowed him to relate to all kinds of people. From the president to a JV player, he could build a friendship with anyone."
— Rollie Massimino, head coach at Northwood University

"Chuck had a great sense of players and their needs. He knew what buttons to push and when to push them and when to leave you alone."
— Julius Erving, "Dr. J," former 76ers star

"There was no better ambassador for the game of basketball than Chuck Daly."
— Mike Krzyzewski, Duke University basketball coach and U.S. Olympics coach, 2008 and 2012

DALY
Wisdom

DALY
Wisdom

LIFE LESSONS
FROM DREAM TEAM COACH
AND HALL-OF-FAMER
CHUCK DALY

by

Pat Williams

with Peggy Matthews Rose

Advantage®

Published by Advantage, Charleston, South Carolina.
Member of Advantage Media Group.

ADVANTAGE is a registered trademark and the Advantage colophon is a trademark of Advantage Media Group, Inc.

Printed in the United States of America.

ISBN: 978-1-59932-163-9
LCCN: 2009911573

This publication is designed to provide accurate and authoritative information in regard to the subject matter covered. It is sold with the understanding that the publisher is not engaged in rendering legal, accounting, or other professional services. If legal advice or other expert assistance is required, the services of a competent professional person should be sought.

Most Advantage Media Group titles are available at special quantity discounts for bulk purchases for sales promotions, premiums, fundraising, and educational use. Special versions or book excerpts can also be created to fit specific needs.

For more information, please write: Special Markets, Advantage Media Group, P.O. Box 272, Charleston, SC 29402 or call 1.866.775.1696.

Visit us online at **advantagefamily**.com

I dedicate this book to the Daly family
—Chuck's wife, Terry, his daughter, Cydney,
his grandchildren Sabrina and Connor, and his brother, Bud.
Thank you for sharing this inspiring coach with all of us.
I hope this book is something you'll treasure
and revisit always.

-Pat Williams

TABLE OF CONTENTS

THE SPARK THAT LIT THIS BOOK

I suppose it is uncommon for the publisher of a book to write a word of tribute, but this book is about an uncommon man—my friend, Chuck Daly.

I first met Coach Daly in 2001, two years after he retired as head coach of the Orlando Magic. He was the keynote speaker at a business breakfast in Greenville, South Carolina. We entered the room at about the same time. I smiled and flashed my Orlando Magic padfolio. He looked at me with a sheepish grin, slapped me on the back, and extended his hand. We chatted for a few minutes and I handed him my business card. Freshly retired, Coach had no business cards, so he generously gave me his cell phone number. He said to let him know if he could do anything to help me.

We were on opposite ends of the professional spectrum at the time. I was a twenty-year-old student/entrepreneur, running a fledgling business from my dorm room at Clemson University. Coach Daly, on the other hand, had just hung up one of the most successful NBA basketball coaching careers to ever grace the hardwood. My life was full of cloud-shaped dreams, while his was full of noisy memories, many with tangible souvenirs—including his Olympic Gold Medal as head coach of the original Dream Team. Why, I asked myself, would a man as accomplished as Chuck Daly have any interest in continuing a conversation with me?

Over the next eight years, Coach and I would swap phone calls every now and then. On two occasions, we managed to catch up for lunch in Detroit. With each visit, whether by phone or in person, Coach shared stories, life lessons, and his inimitable "pearls of wisdom." He was always more than generous with his time and knowledge.

In our final two conversations, Coach and I discussed at length the prospect of working together to write and publish a book. When I asked him his timeline, he looked at me, flashed that classic Daly grin, and said, "Adam, I'm seventy-six. At this point in my life, every day is a gift."

For no good reason, the book project never materialized. When Chuck died, I was immediately convicted and not sure what to do. Chuck was gone and now the book would never be written.

I contacted my friend Pat Williams, who had known Coach Daly for more than forty years, to share my grief and ask his advice. "What could we do?" I asked. And Pat—the man of a million book ideas—came through once again. I was elated when Pat agreed to take on this project. That Coach Daly book would happen, after all.

And what a creative way to approach Chuck Daly's story—through his well known "Chuckisms." So while this is not the book Chuck and I set out to do—Coach was simply too humble to allow a book to be published with the title Daly Wisdom—the gems you're about to add to your personal treasure chest are pure Chuck Daly, through and through. Told through the memories of Chuck's many friends and associates, you'll find a virtual roadmap of wisdom pouring out on every page.

Pull out a pen as you read. Mark favorite stories; highlight those places that make you laugh, tear up, or think—and you'll find many. Share what you're reading with others and give them a dose of *Daly Wisdom* too.

If I could summarize the one thing Coach taught me above anything else, I would use the words of the poet Henry Wadsworth Longfellow: "Give what you have to somebody; it may be better than you think."

May the principles contained in this book enrich your life in the same positive way that Chuck Daly enriched mine. Coach, we finally got the book done.

With Great Enthusiasm & Spirit!

Adam D. Witty

Founder & Chief Executive Officer

Advantage Media Group®

Charleston, South Carolina

January 2010

Chuck Daly died on May 9, 2009—and for a moment the world of basketball stopped. On hearing the news, NBA Commissioner David Stern told ESPN, the "void left by his death will never be filled." But Chuck Daly was more than a great basketball coach. He was known by many names. It's an honor to have this book introduced to you by the only person who called him Daddy.

FOREWORD

He was my hero. To me, he was on a pedestal so high it was like the sun shone only on him. He was magical to me . . . he could do anything.

He showed me the ways of the world. He taught me to treat everyone I meet with respect, and to live my life with honesty and integrity. He taught me that family comes first, but also that friends can become family.

My father was not someone who gave out compliments freely, so when he bestowed one on you, you knew it was from the heart. He was a man's man with a sometimes gruff exterior. But for all that, it was obvious to everyone how deeply he loved my mother and me.

My parents were married for almost fifty-three years. They weathered many storms and celebrated more accomplishments than most people will ever experience.

Yet for all the love he had for Mom and me, there were two special people who completely stole his heart: their names are Sabrina and Connor. In my father's eyes, my greatest accomplishment was presenting him with grandchildren. He was so proud to be their Papa. No longer did he call to ask how I was doing or if I needed anything. It was all about his grandchildren. They could do no wrong in his eyes. Nothing was too good for them.

I remember the time Daddy bought Connor his first suit. Of course, Chuck Daly's grandson had to be impeccably dressed at all times. But Connor was less than a year old—he hadn't even started walking! Daddy just looked at me, beaming, and said, "Whatever. He looks great, doesn't he?"

Sabrina and Connor did not know him as Coach or Hall of Famer. They only knew him as their Papa—the Papa who took them golfing and sneaked in ice cream and cookies when their mom wasn't around. He showed them how to shoot hoops in the driveway and how to throw a football. He was ecstatic when Sabrina took up golf lessons—his passion outside of basketball. I thank God every day that my children had such a special connection to my father, their Papa.

My father leaves a legacy that will stand the test of time. His professional accomplishments are extraordinary, but it is his personal achievements we will carry in our hearts forever. He loved his family fiercely and the friendships he made over the years filled his heart with true happiness. My father was loved by so many people.

I'm grateful our friend Pat Williams has written this book, filled with my father's familiar and best-loved "isms" and the stories of so many who knew him. May they become part of your life too, so that his true legacy will impact our world for many years to come.

Sabrina and Connor, I hope you'll read this book—and meet your amazing Papa as so many others knew him.

– Cydney Daly

INTRODUCTION:
DALY MEMORIES

I'll never forget my introduction to Chuck Daly.

It was February 1965, and I had just started my professional sports career. I was all of twenty-four years old and had been named general manager of the Philadelphia Phillies farm club in Spartanburg, South Carolina. A month earlier, I'd had to make a big decision: did I want to be a sports executive or a broadcaster? I elected the former, with the idea of keeping my hand in broadcasting during the off-season.

I graduated from Wake Forest in 1962. During the '65-'66 season I broadcast their football and basketball games. One night I was barking out a home game from the coliseum in Winston-Salem, North Carolina. I'm sure I was making it sound like the greatest sporting event of all time. Little did I know that Vic Bubas, head coach at Duke, and his young assistant, Chuck Daly, were en route by automobile from Durham, North Carolina, to scout the game. Caught in traffic, they'd missed the start of the game and were listening to my broadcast on the car radio.

The next day, back at the ballpark in Spartanburg, I picked up a ringing phone. It was Vic Bubas. They'd heard me on the radio, he said, and liked my style. Would I be interested in calling some Duke games?

Would I?!

Vic Bubas was just about the hottest name in college basketball then and I was thrilled over the next couple of seasons to announce the play-by-play for a number of Duke games. On occasion, I traveled with the team—and that's how I met Chuck Daly.

In a word, the best way to describe Chuck was—dazzling. Tall. Movie star handsome. Hair perfectly coiffed. Dressed to the nines. Everything matched perfectly. Add a touch of designer cologne and Chuck was indeed a sight—a complete package of elegant style. He was also a terrific basketball coach and everyone who met him predicted a very bright future as a head coach.

Chuck eventually left Duke to become the head coach at Boston College. He wasn't there long before taking over as head coach at the University of Pennsylvania. That's where our paths crossed again.

I'd left baseball in 1968 to enter the NBA, and in the summer of 1974 was named general manager of the Philadelphia 76ers. With Chuck coaching in the city at Penn, our paths crossed fairly regularly.

In the fall of 1977, the 76ers made a coaching change, naming Billy Cunningham as head coach. Cunningham's first request was that we pursue Chuck Daly as his number one assistant. Chuck's season at Penn was just weeks away when I went to visit him at the Palestra. Thankfully, entering the NBA appealed to him. He was definitely interested. So we structured a deal, if I'm remembering correctly, for about $32,000 a year. Not a bad salary . . . thirty-five years ago! And with that, Chuck Daly's NBA career was launched.

He stayed with us for four seasons, until he was hired as head coach of the Cleveland Cavaliers. That turned out to be a short stay, and soon he was back working on Philadelphia's broadcasting team.

At age fifty-two, it appeared as if Chuck's coaching career was just about over—until the Detroit Pistons gave him another chance in 1983. The rest, as they say, is history.

To that date, the Pistons had never had two straight winning seasons. Under Chuck's leadership, they had nine, including back-to-back NBA championships in 1989 and 1990. Then in 1992 he was chosen to head the United States' first Olympic basketball "Dream Team." He earned himself a plaque in the Basketball Hall of Fame.

I was reunited with Chuck once again for two more seasons when he took the reigns as head coach of the Orlando Magic in 1997-98 and 1998-99. What a great opportunity those two years gave me to affirm what I'd already learned about this remarkable man.

Chuck possessed a unique quality called wisdom. He had an ability to analyze any situation and capture it in a few words that went right to the heart of the matter. These pithy little insights became known as "Chuckisms."

As my public speaking career grew and I began addressing the corporate community on leadership and teamwork, I found myself quoting Chuck repeatedly. His "Chuckisms" worked their way into my messages easily, as often as quotes from greats like John Wooden, Vince Lombardi, and other legendary coaches.

When Chuck passed away from pancreatic cancer in May of 2009, a booklet was handed out at his funeral consisting of a handful of his priceless "Chuckisms." As I took it all in, I thought, *Chuck's insights need to be passed around in a wider circle.*

That's what this book is all about.

I devoted several months to tracking down the people closest to Chuck to get their favorites—and the list kept growing and growing. The end result is this little treasure trove of expressions Chuck delivered regularly, pithy life lessons he imparted into so many lives around him. I am pleased now to pass them on to you—fifty-two hard-hitting, fast-paced "Chuckisms." They are paired with a brief explanation of what the "ism" meant to Chuck, along with memories from those who knew him. More importantly, I share how to apply these "Chuckisms" in your own field of endeavor.

Far more than a sports book, this is a book about leadership, success, and making the most of every opportunity you have. I wish Chuck had written this book himself—but this is the next best thing.

-Pat Williams
Orlando, Florida
January 2010

CHAPTER 1:
LET LEADERS LEAD

CHUCKISM #1: PLAYERS PLAY, COACHES COACH, BUS DRIVERS DRIVE THE BUS

So often in professional sports, people are jumping across the lines trying to encroach on other people's turf. Chuck used this phrase repeatedly over the years, because that's how he saw it: tend to your own field. Stick close to your own knitting.

He had a great way of bringing people face-to-face with their own limitations. If a staffer complained about a player, Chuck might retort, "You're no bargain, either!" How do you argue with that?

When you have a situation where the owner wants to be in the locker room delivering the pre-game talks, or when the general manager thinks he knows more about coaching the team than the coach does, it becomes a nightmare scene. Nobody wins.

So owners, you provide the financial resources, hire the best people, empower them, let them do their jobs, and be supportive. General managers, your job is to scout, work the trade lines, provide talent, sign players, and manage the salary cap. But once the season begins, Chuck said, let the coaches coach, the players play, and the bus drivers drive.

Everybody's job is important. If the bus driver has to get the team to the airport and doesn't know the directions or gets lost or is late—you don't have a smooth functioning operation. By the same token, the bus driver does not need to act like the owner.

Longtime Detroit sports columnist Charlie Vincent said of Chuck, "He knew how to handle his men. He knew he was smarter than his players, but he never made them feel that way . . . Chuck picked his spots when to really press on the guys. He knew that 100 games was a long grind and you had to be selective."

Chuck understood that everyone had a role to play. He knew it had to be their own role and not someone else's, or the result would be chaos and failure. He set the example by mastering his own role.

"When he was at Penn, Chuck Daly was the first coach I remember who included the assistant coaches in his huddles during timeouts. He was the ultimate players coach," said longtime Philadelphia sports-writer Jack Scheuer.

Chuck knew a coach had to give his players a balanced life. New Jersey Nets trainer Tim Walsh, who worked for Chuck in Orlando, recalls, "Chuck believed that it was always important not to over-train the players. Sometimes less is more with practice. They need their rest so they will be as fresh as possible for the game."

Charlie Vincent remembers when Chuck "would get ready to put Dennis Rodman in the game. He'd look him in the eye and hold on to his jersey and instruct him, 'Dennis, don't think!' He knew Dennis was an instinctive player and that's how Chuck would motivate him."

"Chuck understood players and how to get the maximum out of each person," said Brendan Suhr, who assisted Chuck in coaching the "Bad Boy" Detroit Pistons in the late 1980s. "He knew Isiah [Thomas] was different than [Bill] Laimbeer and that Laimbeer was different than Rodman. Chuck knew how to get the most out of each guy without disrespecting the others."

Chuck coached and let players like Rodman play. It's the secret that brought him two NBA titles and that choice role with the first Olympic Dream Team. "I'm a pretty good coach when I've got good players," he said. Coach Daly was a "team player" of the highest order.

Isiah Thomas told ESPN.com, "He was coaching all of us until the day he died. He was a wonderful, wonderful human being and a great mentor, a great friend" (http://sports.espn.go.com/nba/news/story?id=4164565).

Vic Bubas coached the Duke University basketball team through ten outstanding seasons, from the 1959-60 season through the 1968-69 season. During that time, he hired Chuck to his first college job. Bubas observed, "When you coach back-to-back NBA titles as Chuck Daly did in Detroit, you have done it at the highest level possible. You are the best of the best."

Everyone has a special skill: figure out what yours is, then own it, hone it, perfect it. And then, as much as possible, stay on your own side of the court. Don't try to do someone else's job. Just be the best you can be at your own.

CHUCKISM # 2:
I'M NOT A COACH, I'M A SALESMAN

Chuck always knew his role was more about convincing people than anything else. When he joined the Magic as head coach in 1997, I was excited to be reunited with him. We were both much deeper into our careers and could talk and analyze life and sports from a much more mature point of view.

One day Chuck, in his typical animated fashion, declared, "I'm not a coach. I'm a salesman!"

"What do you mean by that, Chuck?" I asked.

"Well, all I do all day long is sell," he said. "I'm selling these players on their role on the team or on the number of shots they'll take or the strategy for the next game—and then I go upstairs and start dealing with the front office. I've got to sell them on why this player isn't working out or why we should be making this trade. And every time I talk to the media, all I'm doing is selling them too. I'm selling them on the progress of the team, our game and season goals, on why I did this and didn't do that in a particular game. I guess I'm selling the media so they'll go out and sell the fans, so they'll be supportive. Sell, sell, sell! That's all I do."

I've thought about that a lot, and I realize Chuck was right. When you get down to it, that's all any of us do. We're all sales people. Kids are selling Mom and Dad on why they should stay up later. Young men are selling young women on why they should go out. Corporations are selling clients on why they need their latest product. With every new book deal, I'm out there selling publishers on why they should print my most recent great idea. And every time I watch President Obama on television, he is selling something: the war in Afghanistan, issues involving our economy, healthcare matters—you name it. The man is a nonstop sales person. If the leader of the free world is our number one salesman, then how about the rest of us? Shouldn't we be equally passionate about our ideas? They all require salesmanship to implement.

I often chuckle when young salespeople say to me, "My goal is to get out of sales so I can go into management." *Buddy*, I am thinking, *when that day comes and you get into management—then you'll* really *have to be a salesperson. And the stakes will be a whole lot higher.*

One way to learn is by studying great models like Chuck Daly. Former Orlando Magic assistant Tom Sterner said, "I've been in the NBA a long time and been around a lot of great coaches. I learned the most from Chuck. He could communicate with NBA players and sell them on what had to be done."

Bob Zuffelato was Chuck's assistant at Boston College for two seasons. "Chuck was a terrific salesman," Bob recalled. "He was a great closer when we were recruiting. If we could get him in front of the kid's family, we'd get him."

Successful lives are built on the non-stop selling of what we believe in. Chuck Daly understood that. He mastered the art. He defined his role as "a selling job, night in and night out. I've had surgery on my right knee," he said, "from bending it a lot."

I like how former Pistons player Kelly Tripucka put it when he said, "Chuck's philosophy was to get his best player to buy into his philosophy. If you can accomplish that, the others will follow what you are trying to do. Things will take care of themselves."

CHUCKISM #3:
I'M NOT A COACH, I'M A TEACHER

Kelly Tripucka knew Coach Daly pretty well. "As a coach," he observed, "Chuck wore many hats. He had a coaching hat, a teacher's hat, a parent hat, a motivator hat. He studied his players and knew the ones you could yell at and the ones who needed a pat on the back." I like that description of Chuck. He always knew which hat to put on and when.

As former Penn assistant coach Ray Carazo put it, "Chuck was tremendous to work for. He told you what he wanted done and then let you do it. When I got the head job at Yale, I was fully equipped—because Chuck had allowed me to handle so much at Penn."

After Chuck had joined the Magic in 1997, I recall an intense discussion between the two of us, triggered by Chuck's equally intense exasperation. This time, he spouted, "I'm not a coach. I'm a *teacher*! All I do all day long is teach. Even though we've got the greatest athletes in the world, their fundamentals are terrible. I've got to teach them the basics of the game. And then I've got to teach them how to play as a unit. Before each game, I'm teaching them about their next opponent. I'm just a lifelong teacher."

Reflecting on the conversation afterwards, I recalled Coach Vince Lombardi's keen observation: "They call it coaching, but it's really teaching."

With those words, Coach Lombardi got directly to the heart of what coaching and leadership are all about. It doesn't matter whether you're coaching a YMCA basketball team as a volunteer or sitting on an NBA bench with the greatest players in the world at your disposal, teaching really is your profession.

As I write this book, legendary coach John Wooden has turned ninety-nine years old. Several years ago, I wrote a book about him called *How to Be Like Coach Wooden* (Health Communications, 2006). I spent four and a-half years wrapped up in his life, doing research for the book. In all that time with him, he never once used the word "coach," but rather the word "teach." It was always about teaching with him. Here's how he would talk: "I was teaching the young men under my supervision how to be good basketball players, but more importantly I tried to teach them how to be good citizens." Leaders teach.

So my recommendation to you is to learn from Chuck Daly and John Wooden. As you look to the future, take heart! Take every opportunity to teach your children, your grandchildren, young people at work, students in the classroom, and players on the field. That's a great personal reminder to me from that discussion with Coach Daly.

By the way, there is a key to being a lifelong teacher: you must be a lifelong learner. President John F. Kennedy once said that learning and leadership are indispensible partners. He was right. Never stop learning. It's the secret to being a great teacher.

One other thing about great teachers: we never forget them. "I loved Coach Daly," former Nets player Derrick Coleman said. "He taught me the game of life." Longtime NBA player P.J. Brown played for Chuck with the New Jersey Nets, and told me that experience changed his life.

During his first year of professional play, Coach Daly asked Brown, "'Rookie, do you want to play for me?' I said, 'Yes, sir.' 'Then come prepared to practice every day,' he said. 'If you want to get into the rotation you've got to earn it.' Chuck taught me how to be a professional during practice and games and off the court as well," Brown remembers. "He expected his players to know they were being paid to be pros. Chuck instilled that in me my first season and I carried that approach for all fifteen years of my career in the NBA. That's why I came to Chuck's funeral in Florida from my home near New Orleans. I had to say good-bye to Coach Daly and thank him one last time."

CHUCKISM #4: THE PLAYERS HAVE TO ALLOW YOU TO COACH THEM

When asked about Chuck Daly's greatest strengths, former Pistons' star Isiah Thomas replied, "Relationships, relationships, relationships." And there's no doubt that Chuck's people skills were one of his greatest leadership attributes. He understood that the day of Attila-the-Hun-style leadership is long past. There's no way you can deal with NBA players and treat them as if they are merely pawns on a chessboard.

Chuck realized you must win the hearts and minds of your players over to your side.

Philadelphia 76ers general manager Eddie Stefanski played for Chuck in the 1970s, when Chuck was head coach at the University of Pennsylvania. Eddie told me, "Chuck made you feel you had won something over on him, but in reality he'd already worked it out in advance. The result was that he got what he wanted . . . and it was the best thing for you too."

Former Pistons center Bill Laimbeer knew that side of Chuck well. "Chuck's approach was come to the gym, work hard, and go home," he said. "Simple, but effective. He knew how to point us in the right direction and get out of the way."

Chuck Daly was an innovative coach, always challenging his players. "Chuck would come up with something new every day," said Bo Outlaw, former Orlando Magic player. "I couldn't keep up with it all."

Chuck would often say, "You gotta know your team." Ronnie Rothstein, an assistant coach for the Detroit Pistons under Chuck, believes that was a key to Chuck's greatness. Chuck studied his players. "What's their mood?" Ronnie said, noting a technique we all can learn. He added, "Can you get on them now, or is it time to back off? Be the world's leading authority on your own squad."

Dr. J—the great Julius Erving—saw Chuck's ability to read his players too. He said, "Chuck had a great sense of players and their needs. He knew what buttons to push and when to push them and when to leave you alone."

Former Magic player Nick Anderson remembers his time with Chuck fondly because of this personal touch. "Chuck believed in me and instilled confidence in my mind," Nick told me. "He was a motivator and believed in giving his players second chances."

Chuck was a born encourager who knew how to cultivate talent and get the most from every player. Matt Harpring, who joined the Magic as a rookie out of Georgia Tech in 1997, played under Chuck for one year. "Chuck was a solid person who cared about his players," Matt remembers. "He didn't spend a lot of time talking to rookies, but he liked my aggressiveness going after offensive boards. One day I was watching film with him after practice, and he said, 'Son, you keep rebounding that way and you'll be in this league as long as you want to be.' I never forgot that."

Matt's fellow rookie teammate, Michael Doleac, remembers a time late in that '97-'98 season when he and Matt were spending time working on their shooting. "Chuck walked the length of the court, and said, 'I see what you're doing. Keep it up.' And then he turned and walked away. I remembered those words from Chuck during my whole ten-year career," Michael said.

"Chuck's practices were usually quick and short. His philosophy was, 'Don't leave it on the practice court. Save it for the game,'" said former Pistons player Adrian Dantley.

"Chuck understood the subtleties of each player and what was best for each guy," notes Wendy Schayes, wife of longtime NBA center Danny Schayes. "He made everyone feel important and valuable."

Dream Team member Patrick Ewing remembers, "Chuck knew how to give his players the proper rest and not kill us in practice. He wasn't one of those coaches who constantly berated his players. Chuck knew how to push the right buttons to get the best out of you."

"Chuck coached each individual personally," said Joe Dumars, a Pistons guard under Chuck. "He knew how to deal with each guy to get the best out of him, and he did it every day."

Chuck was very focused when it came to understanding the players' personalities and what motivated them," remembers Bob Vander Weide, President and CEO of the Orlando Magic. "He knew how to connect with them through wise and passionate words. As a result, he took the players to a higher level of consistent performance."

Pistons broadcaster George Blaha agrees that Chuck took time to understand the mentality of his players. "The players were saying, 'We've got a really cool coach and we like playing for him.'"

Chuck modeled coaching for other coaches as well as for his players. P. J. Carlesimo, who served as an assistant coach with Chuck on the 1992 Olympic Dream Team, told me, "Chuck was a mentor to me and I studied him closely. He knew how to get the best out of his players and not get caught up in the personality conflicts so many of us couldn't avoid. He was a players' coach in the truest sense of the word."

Have you worked for a coach or a boss you enjoyed working for? That seems to be a rarity in our culture these days. Practice being someone your team members admire and respect—someone they like playing for.

If Chuck believed in you, he supported you. NBA TV analyst Doug Collins played and coached for many years and was on our 76ers team when Chuck was an assistant coach. He recalls, "Years later when

I became the Pistons' head coach, Chuck was the one who put in the key word of recommendation for me with their brass."

Chuck's authenticity both on and off the basketball court showed a key leadership quality. It's important to be the same person everywhere you go. Too many attain a position of power and begin to shut out old friends and associates, as if they're too high up for them. That was *not* Chuck Daly.

Chuck's good friend John Ginopolis, a restaurant owner in Michigan, told me, "Chuck never realized how big he was. He was appreciative of all the good things in his life and took the time to talk to people."

Rick Carlisle, who is currently head coach of the Dallas Mavericks, was an assistant coach under Chuck when he coached the New Jersey Nets. Rick explained to me, "Along with John Wooden and Pete Newell, Chuck was basketball's most humble icon. There's never been a more brilliant man, or one who took himself less seriously, than Chuck Daly."

My favorite story here again involves Coach John Wooden. One day, at the height of Coach Wooden's success at UCLA, he called the home of longtime college scout Bill Bertka.

"I'm sorry, Bill is out of the office," answered Mrs. Bertka.

"Would you tell him John Wooden called?" Coach asked. "That's W-O-O-D-E-N."

"Coach," replied Mrs. B, "I *know* who you are."

No matter where you are in the line-up—whether you're the head coach or the water boy—you've got to develop this critical people skill called humility. Chuck Daly saw it when those players, who could have been strutting their hot stuff and glorying in their six-figure salaries, recognized his position and let him coach them. What area of your life needs that spirit of humility today? Better yet, who needs to see it in you?

CHUCKISM #5: EVERY DAY IS A CRISIS. MY JOB IS TO LAND THE PLANE SAFELY

I've heard it said that coaching in the NBA is like a nervous breakdown with paychecks. Chuck said to me on a number of occasions, "I could have a confrontation every minute of every day with somebody. I could get into it with the players during practice, or with the general manager, or opposing coaches, or the media. In fact I could go to battle endlessly with writers and broadcasters over something they wrote that I disagreed with.

"But I learned early in my coaching career," Chuck added, "that I was like the pilot of an airplane. The pilot's job is to navigate that plane through smooth weather conditions as well as stormy, turbulent weather. If he is flying from New York to Los Angeles, the only thing that matters is bringing the plane down safely at LAX. Nobody cares about the storms he has to deal with en route."

Howard Garfinkel, founder and director of the 5 Star Basketball Camp in Briarcliff Manor, New York, observed, "I judge coaches by how they coach at the end of a game in a tight situation. With three minutes to go, Chuck Daly was the master. His moves were brilliant. No one was better. When the pressure was intense, Chuck was deadly."

Navigating a plane safely onto the tarmac requires the foresight to see obstacles before you fly smack-dab into them. On the court, Chuck was a flight plan master. Julius Erving—Dr. J who played so well for our 76ers team—remembers Chuck as a man with "the amazing ability to see things coming down the pike in advance. He knew how to prevent molehills from becoming mountains."

Bob Zuffelato, who assisted Chuck at Boston College, remarked, "Chuck had a real feel for what was ahead and could lay things out in his mind."

Former Philadelphia broadcaster Neil Funk added, "Chuck could see way ahead in a game by what had happened prior. He could predict in the first quarter what was going to happen in the fourth quarter. Invariably, he'd be accurate."

Navigating that plane also requires intense focus along with the ability to put the mission into perspective. While serving as an assistant coach with the 1992 Dream Team, P. J. Carlesimo observed, "Chuck was always looking at the big picture and, thus, was able to avoid getting sidetracked by the peripheral issues."

"The greatest tribute ever paid to Chuck Daly was being named Head Coach of the 1992 Olympic Dream Team," said *Boston Globe* columnist Bob Ryan. "Here's why he was chosen:

1. A complete knowledge of the game.

2. He had the perfect temperament to handle the stars.

3. Chuck was always in control.

4. He was a pragmatist and knew what to do to get the job done. His mission was to steer the ship of state in the proper manner.

"It was not about wins and losses because the USA team was going to win. Chuck got what it was all about."

Chuck believed that as a coach he was in the same seat as that pilot. If you can't handle bad news, you probably should get out of the coaching business, because generally there's going to be more negative than positive news.

General Colin Powell has an interesting take on this: "Leadership," he has said, "is solving problems. When people stop bringing you their problems, you're through as a leader."

So leaders, is your life full of problems? Crises? Storms? If so, you're in great shape. Your job is secure. You're not going anywhere.

CHUCKISM #6: THE BEST ASSET A COACH HAS IS SELECTIVE HEARING

When Chuck was coaching the Detroit Pistons, he had a wonderful asset sitting on his bench named Vinnie "Microwave" Johnson. He would come off the bench firing and could heat up an offense instantaneously. Also highly emotional, Johnson didn't like to come out of the game—particularly when he was "hot." But his primary function was as that spark plug off the bench.

Vinnie would come out of the game at just the right time, and when he did, he'd come storming down the bench, muttering a blue streak. Chuck would simply ignore him, let him cool down, and put him back in again at the right time. Chuck's philosophy was that selective hearing was a coach's greatest asset.

I had an interesting discussion on that topic with former NBA coach-turned sports analyst Hubie Brown one day. Hubie had worked with Chuck at Duke University. Chuck was great, he told me, at not over-reacting when he heard something inflammatory. "I could never do that," said Hubie. "I would force a confrontation right on the spot if a player said something I didn't like. It would have been more helpful if my selective hearing was better."

One night when Chuck was coaching the Magic, he had a dilemma with the volatile guard Vern Maxwell. Chuck leaned over to one of his assistants, Eric Musselman, and said, "We've got to get Maxwell out of there."

"But he'll come ranting and raving in front of our bench and the whole crowd will see it," Musselman objected.

Chuck thought about it. "OK," he said, "we'll take him out. But we'll remove him at the next time out. That way nobody will see it."

Former Pistons executive Harry Hutt remembers a night toward the end of a season. The players were tired and ready for playoffs to start. "In this particular game, the Pistons are down by fifteen at the half," Hutt related. "Near the end of halftime, Chuck gathers the players in a huddle and is somewhat animated—lecturing them about their lack of effort and their resulting poor play."

About a minute in, an angry voice let out a loud invective (let the reader imagine). "Everybody wheels around and it's Dennis Rodman, visibly upset," Harry went on. "Chuck kicks into selective hearing loss, continues talking, and Rodman shouts out again. Chuck ignores Rodman, continues his speech and then gives the old, '1-2-3, let's go!'—acting like nothing happened.

"Somehow the selective hearing loss worked, because, in the second half, the Pistons rallied for a last minute win and Rodman was sensational. Because of Chuck's 'hearing loss,' what could have been an unpleasant scuffle turned into another win for the Pistons. He knew it wasn't personal with Dennis. He was just an intense competitor who wanted to win. And Rodman always referred to Chuck as his surrogate father."

Former Penn assistant Bob Weinhauer concurs regarding Chuck's selective hearing ability. "Chuck believed you had to learn how to hear what you wanted to hear and see what you wanted to see," Bob told me. "You had to overlook certain things and not create too many crises unnecessarily. However, Chuck always had good discipline and complete control. That is a real art. He had the respect of his players all the time and that came by how he carried himself. He was firm yet fair at the same time. He wasn't getting into you. Chuck coached his personality and his philosophy."

Duke University coach Mike Krzyzewski has never forgotten this advice from Chuck: "To be a good NBA coach, you need to be hard of hearing and have poor eyesight." In Chuck's case, the memory, hearing, and eyesight "impairment" was purely intentional.

Learning the art of selective hearing saved Chuck from many an embarrassing, heated, and undoubtedly public episode. Can anyone out there relate to moments like this? Mom and Dad? Los Angeles freeway driver? Leaders in board meetings? Let this "Chuckism" inspire you to tune out what doesn't ultimately matter and achieve your goals in creative new ways.

CHUCKISM #7: THAT'S MY JOB

One day, Chuck was conducting a press conference that was turning especially touchy and uncomfortable. His public relations director had suggested that Chuck could avoid handling the event and the team would cover for him. "No," Chuck responded. "That's my job." Chuck understood responsibility. Leadership was a privilege and calling he firmly grasped.

As a coach, Chuck also realized that part of his responsibility was raising up the next generation of leaders. Longtime fellow coach and broadcaster Jack Ramsay describes Chuck's best talent as that of "getting his players to buy into his system and take on some leadership responsibility of the team—especially Isiah Thomas and Bill Laimbeer. Those two helped ride herd on their teammates and got them to toe the line."

We are living today in an age of deflected responsibility. Leaders across the nation make decisions every day. If they work out, they can't wait to take credit. If they don't work out, Leader X develops a case of instant amnesia and has zero recall of what transpired. And then the next step is to hire a spin-doctor to help further extricate our "leader" from this mess he wants no part of. That never happened with Chuck Daly.

One of my favorite examples of responsibility in leadership took place on June 5, 1944. General Dwight Eisenhower and his military team had laid out plans for a major invasion of Normandy and now it was the night before they would execute the plan. For Ike, it was as if the weight of the world was literally on his shoulders. This was his military campaign, and even with all the planning there was no way to predict how it would turn out. To make matters worse, the weather had taken a hard turn for the worse. On that night, the night before the D-Day invasion that history tells us launched the end of World War II, Eisenhower wrote a note in which he took full responsibility if the campaign failed. It didn't, of course. The war was won and the world should be thankful we had a capable leader in command. Eisenhower understood Chuck Daly's philosophy: "No, that's *my* job."

Will you agree with me that the world needs more leaders who live by this principle? More than that, will you be one of them?

CHUCKISM #8:
THIS ISN'T MY FIRST RODEO

A video interviewer once asked Chuck Daly what advice he had to share with his audience. Chuck responded with his typical air of humility, looking somewhat embarrassed at the question. "Well," he began, "it's not my first rodeo, after all. I've been around the block a few times." How typically Chuck Daly—not bragging about his accomplishments, just resting on his experience.

My daughter Karyn lives in Nashville and is working her way into the country music scene as a singer and songwriter. I hope one day Karyn can write and record a song rivaling my all time favorite tune. A deep-voiced star named Vern Gosdin rumbles out this country classic: "This ain't my first rodeo. This ain't the first time this old cowboy's been throwed. This ain't my first dog and pony show. This ain't my first rodeo."

There really is no substitute for experience. You have got to pay your dues. Successful people learn their craft from the ground up.

Chuck Daly's background—his rodeo ropes, if you will—was fascinating and somewhat untypical for coaches in the NBA. He started out as a high school teacher and coach working in small towns in Pennsylvania. In 1963, he was hired by Coach Vic Bubas at Duke University. By his mid-thirties, he'd paid his dues as a freshman coach, top recruiter, varsity assistant—you name it. Finally, he got the head-coaching job at Boston College. He was forty years old at the time.

By the time we hired him to work with the Philadelphia 76ers, Chuck was forty-seven. He didn't become a head coach in the NBA until he was in his early fifties, and it was a decade later when he was picked to head the first Olympic Dream Team in 1992.

What was it that made Chuck such a valuable "rodeo cowboy"? Experience mattered, of course, but along the way Chuck learned how to teach the game of basketball. He learned how to deal with all the situations that would come up later in his career on a world stage. The whole art of coaching became second nature for him.

"Chuck Daly had great insights," concluded Andy Dolich, formerly of the Memphis Grizzles, "because he'd been around the block in this business."

Chuck had indeed been around the block a time or two. He'd learned the game from the ground up and coached at every level. Chuck's grammar was a bit better than Vern Gosdin's, but the lesson is clear: There's no quick way to the top. No elevator to the Hall of Fame. You've got to pay your dues.

CHAPTER 2:
WITHOUT TEAMWORK, YOU'VE GOT NOTHIN'

CHUCKISM #9: THEY ALL WANT THREE THINGS— 48 MINUTES, 48 SHOTS AND $48 MILLION

When game time comes around, every professional player wants one thing: to be on the court for a full forty-eight minutes.

Former Pistons player Rick Mahorn recalls, "Chuck Daly coached and led by example. He explained to us that if you will work hard in practice, you will earn your minutes during the games. It was that simple."

"Here is what I learned about coaching from Chuck:

- Be dedicated.

- Be committed.

- Be a student of the game.

- Keep learning every day, no matter how long you've been a coach."

Chuck had the most wonderful way of reducing complex issues to their very simplest form. He was once asked what it was like coaching NBA players. He thought for a minute and said, "Oh, it's not very complicated. I could keep them all happy if I could just get them forty-eight minutes of playing time, forty-eight shots a night, and forty-eight million dollars in their contract."

I remember laughing when I heard that analysis, but it is right to the point.

Former West-German Chancellor Konrad Adenauer had this philosophy: "As soon as you are complicated you are ineffectual." It's important to be simple and direct in communicating with others. We tend to speak in such confusing and bewildering monologues and dialogues these days that nobody knows what we're trying to say. Keep it simple, so anyone can get it. Former General Electric CEO Jack Welch believes you should be able to explain what you want to strangers at a cocktail party in less than a minute. That's a great tip.

I remember a phone conversation I had one day with the legendary Bob Shepherd, the longtime public announcer voice at Yankee Stadium—the man former Yankee great Reggie Jackson described as having the voice of God. Over the phone I asked Bob, a speech teacher in his real profession, what he considered the three keys to being a good public speaker. He intoned:

"1. Be clear. 2. Be concise. 3. Be correct."

When I hung up, I thought, *Coach Daly would buy that philosophy 100%.*

Chuck realized that keeping his team motivated was paramount. "Play forty-eight minutes," he was known to shout—to encourage them to play every minute of the game.

What does it take to keep your team motivated? Be clear, concise, and correct in communicating it. Keep them focused on their forty-eight minutes, on what it takes to win the game. Be dedicated, committed, and a student of your business. And do one other thing Chuck did: keep learning every day.

CHUCKISM #10:
HANG AROUND, GUYS. HANG AROUND

Brendan Malone, currently an assistant with the Orlando Magic, was one of Chuck's assistants with the great Piston teams of the late 1980s. He frequently tells the story of Chuck on the bench in those close games—the ones that would come right down to the wire.

"His mantra to the players was 'Hang around, guys. Hang around,'" Malone said. "In other words, keep playing. You don't know what's going to happen, so don't let up. Stay in the game. The other team may self-destruct. The referee may give us a key call. If you hang around, you give yourself a chance to win the game."

I've thought often about that quote. I think it's a key to succeeding in life. I love to study the lives of great leaders and highly successful people. I'm convinced we never should have heard of any of them. George Washington lost more battles than he won in the Revolutionary War. Abraham Lincoln had so many things going against him, he never should have left Illinois. Franklin D. Roosevelt suffered such a debilitating attack of polio it should have taken him off the scene forever. Winston Churchill battled severe bouts of depression. One of my heroes, Walt Disney, went bankrupt twelve times and had two nervous breakdowns.

None of these people knew Chuck Daly, but they all practiced his philosophy: Hang around, hang around. You never know what will happen.

A few years ago, I attended a San Diego Padres game with my friend Dr. David Jeremiah. David is a busy man. The pastor of a large church in San Diego County, he also writes, has a radio and television ministry, and travels extensively.

"David," I asked, "at what point do you plan to retire as a pastor?"

"I have no such plans, Pat," he replied. "Everything I do triggers from my preaching in the pulpit." And then he said something that really hit home: "You never want to be a former anything. People forget you real quick."

The last time I saw Chuck Daly was in the fall of 2008. There was no hint or shadow then of the pancreatic cancer that would take his life in May 2009. He was working at the time as a consultant for the Memphis Grizzlies and had no plans for slowing down. One day Chuck was in Orlando, so we had lunch together and I shared with him what David Jeremiah had told me. "I like that," Chuck said. It really went hand-in-glove with his philosophy, "Hang around, guys. Hang around."

There should never come a point in your life where you say, "It's over. There's nothing left to do." Walt Disney invented a word that also fits this "Chuckism": he called it *stick-to-it-ivity*. That word is not in the dictionary, but it should be.

So whether you call it perseverance, resolve, doggedness, tenacity, stubbornness, single-mindedness, staying power, or determination—it comes down to Chuck's phrase: Hang around, hang around. It's the best way to make sure you'll never be a former *anything*.

CHUCKISM #11: YOU GET PAID TO PLAY
EIGHTY-TWO NIGHTS A YEAR

The NBA season is a marathon. Players work on their weaknesses during the summer months, go into attack mode in September, then training camp heats up in October, and at last the regular season starts around November 1. From that moment, it grinds on for eighty-two games, until mid-April. After that, the playoffs start—and that's a whole other season unto itself. The two finalists duke it out until the middle of June. That's a long, long trek. So it's very easy and tempting for a player to take some nights off, shift into cruise control, and be careless in his approach.

Chuck wouldn't stand for those mid-season mental vacations. He was adamant that his players put out a maximum effort every night.

Former Magic player Darrell Armstrong recalls, "Chuck put an emphasis on the players to be ready. He expected it and that made them grow up quickly. If you caught on, Chuck would play you, no matter where you ranked on the team. If you didn't catch on, you'd sit on the bench. Chuck taught us to be professional as players and people. Be ready to play every game—that's what you get paid for."

When you take the average player's salary, which is sizeable even at the rookie levels, and divide it by eighty-two—that's a hefty per-game paycheck. Failure to perform at the highest level really is cheating. Players who allow themselves to become lazy are holding out on their employer, their teammates, and the ticket buying public.

Your job may not be as visible as that of an NBA player, but the principle is the same. Divide 300 workdays into your salary. Is your employer getting his money's worth from your daily performance? How about your coworkers and your family? Chuck reminds all of us that you've got to come prepared to play every day.

Coach John Wooden, one of my mentors, puts it more succinctly: "Make each day your masterpiece." Do that and you can't go wrong.

By the way, Chuck also knew how to make the most of his downtime over the season. His assistant Eric Musselman remembers, "After games on the road, Chuck was in a frantic rush to get out of there and off to the airport. I once asked him why that was so important to him. He said, 'We can save twenty minutes, and over eighty-two games that is a lot of shuteye. It's a long season and every minute of sleep counts.'"

CHUCKISM #12:

OURS IS A SUFFERING BUSINESS

In 1977, I was general manager of the Philadelphia 76ers. At the start of that year we made a coaching change and Billy Cunningham was named head coach. It was Billy's first experience coaching and he asked for Chuck Daly, then coach at the University of Pennsylvania, as his assistant. So we hired Chuck that year. It was his first NBA job. The Sixers had a strong team, led by the great Julius Erving, and were favored to win the NBA championship. The regular season went well, but the playoffs didn't. We ended up losing to the then Washington Bullets in a crushing game-six defeat on their court. To this day, it remains one of my most painful NBA losses.

The next day I was back in my Philadelphia office when Chuck walked over to my desk and simply said, "Ours is a suffering business."

"What do you mean, Coach?" I asked.

"Everybody goes home suffering except one," he said. "The teams that didn't make the playoffs are suffering, and the teams that didn't make the finals suffer most of all. It's a suffering business." With that, Coach Daly walked out of my office . . . I guess to do more suffering.

We all have setbacks and defeats throughout our lifetimes; maybe more losses than wins. I think Chuck's message is this: *Enjoy the good times. Rejoice over your victories. But learn from those suffering times.*

The best piece of advice I ever got came from Dr. Warren Wiersbe, former pastor of Moody Church in Chicago, in the midst of some suffering times I had when I was general manager of the Bulls. Pastor

Wiersbe reminded me, "Don't waste your sufferings. Keep learning. Keep growing. Let those suffering times strengthen you and prepare you for a more productive life of service."

No matter what business you are in, at the end of the day, someone will win and someone will lose. Chuck Daly realized it's the nature of all businesses. You will know times of suffering. Because "ours is a suffering business." Don't waste your tough times. Keep growing. Make your next season your best.

CHUCKISM #13: WE HAVE TOO MANY MEETINGS IN BASKETBALL AND THEY WILL KILL YOU. YOU CAN TALK TOO MUCH—PLAYERS GET TIRED OF YOUR VOICE

Chuck had an interesting philosophy about meetings. He said, "Every time-out during a game is a meeting. Every pregame discussion is a meeting. Every halftime is a meeting. Every practice session is another meeting. Players can only handle so much and they will start tuning you out."

Former Magic assistant Tom Sterner remembers a meeting one morning in New York before a game with the Knicks: "We were in a conference room on the twentieth floor overlooking the river. I was delivering the scouting report when Chuck, who was standing by the window, starts yelling, 'Hey, hey, over here. Everybody to the window.' The players didn't know what to think. Chuck pointed to the river and said, 'See that ferry? That's the one I took from New Jersey when I was coaching the Nets.' That was the end of the meeting. Chuck told me later, 'I thought they were getting bored and needed a shake up. They'd had enough.' Well, we beat the Knicks that night and I got a lesson from Chuck about studying people and knowing what makes them tick."

Coach Eric Musselman was an assistant with the Magic when Chuck was head coach. Musselman recalls, "Chuck believed strongly in the importance of letting your assistants have a voice. He told me, 'Don't call time outs unnecessarily unless you have a serious message to deliver to the troops. They've already heard you too much.'"

"Chuck taught me a great leadership principle," said Pistons executive Dan Hauser. "Sometimes the fewer words we speak the better. Over one-hundred-plus games, the players can get tired of your voice. Chuck would let the assistants talk during practice, during half times, and during pre-game sessions. The players will turn you off if you talk ceaselessly. Then when you do talk, you have their attention. The bottom line—let others speak."

There's a good lesson here for parents: Don't talk your children to death. Just like NBA players, they will tune you out—and some of your best parental speeches will end up on the locker room floor. Pick your spots wisely.

Don't be afraid to let others speak into your kids' lives—teachers, coaches, pastors. It's amazing how often those voices reinforce the lessons you want your children to learn in ways they will actually *get*, and then remember for years to come.

When you do speak, make sure it's the right message at the right time. Timing is critical for maximum impact. It's true that the less said delivers the biggest wallop. Give it a try, and see what happens.

Oh, and about all those meetings: do you really need them? If they're taking away from productivity, maybe you don't. I'm not knocking the pow-wows. We all need to see each other's faces now and then and know that we're on the same page. But perhaps one or two fewer "time outs" would suffice.

CHUCKISM #14: CHERISH AND SAVOR EVERY DAY YOU'RE IN THE NBA

Lonnie Cooper is an attorney in Atlanta who represents a multitude of NBA coaches. For years he was Chuck's attorney too. Lonnie told me, "Chuck never forgot where he came from. He was always a high school coach at heart. He cared so much about people succeeding."

Chuck's "inner" high school coach understood that even at the professional level, practice was needed every day for a team to succeed. "Chuck didn't run long practices," former Piston Kelly Tripucka told me. "He kept it simple and wanted his players to have fun. They respected him for that. His philosophy of practice was 'let's get it done and move on.'" Chuck Daly loved being a coach, and when he made it to the big leagues he was in heaven.

Chuck spent the early part of his career rattling round in school buses, small high school gyms, and later grinding it out on the college-recruiting trail. I think Chuck always had a hard time even grasping where he ended up—coaching at the highest level, flying on chartered airplanes, staying in five-star hotels, coaching the first Olympic Dream Team. I imagine he had to pinch himself a lot of the time.

He learned how to adapt himself quickly to the NBA environment, where the competition can eat you alive if you let it. "Chuck told me when he took the Orlando Magic coaching job, he asked for $301 in per diem," said Don Shane from WXYZ in Detroit. "I asked him why and he said, 'That's one more dollar than Pat Riley.' Pat was coaching the Miami Heat then, but Chuck had been competing with him for a long time over the years." Chuck understood that the best way to deal with rivalry is through good humor and good sportsmanship.

Chuck fit the NBA better than a brand new Nike Air sports shoe. He developed friendships that served him well to his last breath. I believe it takes a special man to attract people that way—a man of integrity and strong character. That was Chuck Daly. As a result of his high standards, he was well-liked and highly admired.

Chuck loved people and enjoyed taking friends to dinner, and even there he did not compromise his standards. George Blaha has broadcast Pistons games since the 1976-77 season. He remembers, "Chuck would go to a *man's* type restaurant, where you'd get lamb chops and lobster, big sliced tomatoes and onions, and where there'd be framed sports photos on the wall. You wouldn't see Chuck at a French restaurant. Chuck had a scouting system in place for the best spots in every city."

Phil Jasner, longtime *Philadelphia Daily News* 76ers beat writer, told me about the day toward the end of Chuck's life when a bunch of his coaching friends went to visit Chuck in the hospital. "They planned to go out for lunch. Around noon, they started to get ready to go when a nurse arrived. 'Mr. Daly,' she said, 'you are not leaving this room!' At that point, Chuck reached into his pocket and pulled out three $100 bills and said to his friends, 'Here, lunch is on me.'"

NBA veteran coach Jack Ramsay told me, "When Billy Cunningham was named the 76ers head coach in 1977, he had never coached anywhere. The smartest thing Billy did was hire Chuck Daly as his assistant. They became a great pair and over the years developed a strong friendship. They ended up living close to each other in south Florida and after Chuck got sick, Billy stepped up to direct Chuck's life. Billy got him to his cancer treatments and helped Chuck make tough life-altering decisions. And, of course, Billy made all the funeral arrangements. It was a quite a story."

Chuck, of course, would remind us often that making our living in this profession really is a blessing and a gift. Joe Dumars, who played on Chuck's championship Pistons teams, remembers the "Chuckism" that went, "Wake up every day and be thankful we get to do this."

I believe Chuck would say that's true for any industry in which you find your fit, be it professional sports, working for a corporation in some capacity, or serving the public through political office. No matter what you're privileged to be doing, never take it for granted. Never think you're due any of these good things. Go about your business everyday with energy and enthusiasm. And be grateful for the opportunity.

None of us are designed to be a lone ranger in life. We need to be part of a team. If you're a stay-at-home mom, what you do in raising your children contributes to making this world a better place for future generations. If you're an empty nester feeling "unneeded"—nothing could be further from the truth. Your rich life experiences, your values and opinions, your knowledge, are all needed by those around you. Actively search for ways to invest back into the culture.

Keep this philosophy from Chuck Daly in mind:

"Having coached at all levels, I know one thing: teams win championships, not individuals. The players must have ability, but it's essential that they perform as a team. They have to be unselfish, and it's hard to find unselfish players."

See yourself as a member of a team. Develop your skills. Determine to be an unselfish player. Teams win championships, not individuals.

CHUCKISM #15:
DIFFERENT TEAM; SAME PROBLEMS

Rick Carlisle joined Chuck Daly's coaching staff in New Jersey in 1993. Chuck had finished a nine-year run with the Pistons, including NBA titles in 1989-90. It would be safe to assume that outsiders would view those great Piston teams as a walk in the park. But Chuck dealt with as many problems as any other coach. After arriving in New Jersey to coach the Nets, then a struggling franchise, he said to Rick one day, "Different team, same problems."

That's one of my favorite "Chuckisms." It's closely linked to "the grass is greener" syndrome. You know the steps: "If I could just work for that *other* company I bet my life would be better; if I could just get out of this marriage and be married to that *other* person I'd have a trouble free life; if we could just live in *another* neighborhood, we'd be much happier; if I could just transfer to that *other* college—I'll bet it's utopian over there."

Chuck reminds all of us that no matter where you go, "you" are along for the ride as well. You can't escape it. Behind closed doors, in the inner sanctum of any organization, you'll find the same problems brewing away.

So don't look for heaven on earth. It doesn't exist. Keep your focus on where you are right now. Zero in on nourishing the grass in your own backyard.

Chuckism #16: Shooting makes up for a multitude of sins

Hubie Brown is a fascinating guy. After a long career as a coach, he's become one of basketballs outstanding TV analysts. Hubie and Chuck Daly first connected at Duke in mid-'60s as assistants under Coach Vic Bubas.

"One day we were standing in front of a recruiting board listing twenty-five prospects under each of the five different positions," Hubie recalls. "All the players can't get into Duke, so Chuck says to me, 'You're in charge of recruiting.' As we discussed recruiting philosophy, Chuck hit me with this one: 'Shooting makes up for a multitude of sins.' In other words, at the end of the day, basketball is about putting the ball in the net. We can dwell so much on weaknesses and faults that we overlook the most important thing: get the ball in the goal. Chuck could always see the big picture and reduce it to its ultimate simplicity. He could see beyond what was happening today. Chuck had a great understanding of offensive basketball. With equal talent, he could get players their best shots."

George Blaha, longtime voice of the Detroit Pistons, remembers, "As a coach, Chuck was very direct—but in a non-threatening way. He had one directive on offense: shoot the ball. He allowed his players to do the things they did best and if you had an open shot and didn't take it, the offense breaks down."

So learn to reduce your task to its lowest common denominator. Keep focusing on the major issues of your situation. It's so easy to get sidetracked and get your eyes pulled off the main highway.

Keep the chief thing the chief thing. Play to your people's strengths. As a leader, get your best people doing what they do best. Let them grow and become all they can be.

Walt Disney identified his best artists and continually challenged them to stretch just a little more out of their comfort zones. As a result, we have a heritage of classic Disney art—both on the screen and in the theme parks—to enjoy. And those artists had lives most of us can only imagine, all because they focused every day on producing the best entertainment experience. Chuck Daly challenged his best players to "move the ball" and produced winning teams.

If you can lead like that, you may become legendary yourself.

CHAPTER 3:
ONLY REAL PEOPLE NEED APPLY

CHUCKISM #17: YOU CAN'T FOOL DOGS, KIDS—OR NBA PLAYERS

There were no airs about Chuck Daly. What you saw was what you got. The word that describes him best is "integrity"—and it's an interesting word. In fact, not long ago the folks at Merriam Webster's online dictionary (www.m-w.com) said it was the most frequently looked up word. Its root word is "integer," and it means *one, whole, undivided,* as in an integrated society. So to Chuck, integrity meant that if you were not the real deal, you'd be unmasked pretty quickly. No point in trying to hide it.

We've heard for years the saying that you can't fool dogs or children. They're great at spotting phonies. So watch how they react to you—it's a pretty good indicator of how purely you're living your life.

Chuck took that thought one step further and added "or NBA players." These professionals easily pick up signs of any coach who's not genuine, who's trying to con you, or who lives by double standards. If your walk and talk are out of alignment, you are done. Chuck understood this truth: Be consistent in how you deal with others, whether they're your star players, the rookies, or the equipment handlers.

Don't be one person at game time and another off the court. Your players can sense right away whether or not you're the real deal.

Don Magnuson and Chuck Daly were high school friends who never lost touch. "Chuck was sixteen when I met him and I was eighteen," said Don. "Over the years he never changed. Despite all the success he had, Chuck remained the same. He came back to Kane, Pennsylvania every year to visit. He never forgot his hometown."

Former Pistons CFO Ron Campbell shared with me a variation on this "Chuckism": "You can't fool the locker room."

"The players know what's going on," Ron observed, "so don't try to con them. Be honest and open with your players because they can tune you out real quickly if you aren't."

Memphis Grizzlies owner Michael Heisley told me, "Chuck would state his position on a matter, but he wouldn't argue with you. He had supreme confidence in his knowledge and ability and that allowed him to be at peace with himself. He didn't want to be someone he wasn't."

That's a secret I believe Chuck understood well and it will take you far as well. Know your game—be confident in what you believe—and stand your ground when you do. You'll always be respected for that. No one will ever think you're a phony when you're honest and firm about what matters most to you. Even dogs, kids, and NBA players will see it.

CHUCKISM #18: STAY OUT OF THE LIMELIGHT BECAUSE IT'S A PLAYERS' LEAGUE

The world of coaching basketball is fascinating. In high school, it's all about the players. High school coaches view themselves as teachers, mentors—as life encouragers. At the college level, the coach becomes the star. If his team is doing well, he's there for the long haul. The program is built around him. Some of the players might be there for a year or two, but the turnover really is constant. The coach, however, remains. He is the focal point.

At the professional level, it reverts to the high school days. Here, the focus is back on the players and the coach has to understand that. Chuck was always advising other coaches, "Don't try to compete with the players for endorsements, commercial activity, or any of that. They see the promotional world as their turf. If, as a coach, you've got a big ego—deal with it quickly. Once the players resent you for being too commercial and too active, they can really lay the wood to you."

"If Chuck saw somebody in the limelight acting improperly in public and not being discreet about it, he'd use this 'Chuckism,'" remembers Ron Campbell, who served as the Pistons CFO in the 1980s. "He would say, 'He thinks he's invisible.'"

Chuck never let himself be fooled by any illusions of fame. He was fully aware that the games were all about the players. New Jersey Nets President Rod Thorn noted, "Chuck Daly was the perfect coach for the '92 Dream Team. His personality didn't intrude on the players and his players loved him for it. Chuck had a good way about him and didn't get caught up in himself. His ego didn't get in the way."

Longtime NBA center Danny Schayes told me, "I loved playing for Chuck Daly the last two years of my career in Orlando. He never got caught up in the drama of being around NBA players. Chuck's entire approach was 'win games and act professional.' He understood how players thought and knew it was important for him to stay above the fray."

Bucky Waters, former coaching associate at Duke University, said, "Chuck Daly was a bright, warm, caring guy. He was very comfortable not being the center of attention. He worked hard at that."

Eric Musselman, a one-time Magic assistant, remembers learning that lesson at a strategic time, shortly after being named head coach of the Golden State Warriors. For the 2002-2003 season, Musselman ended up second to San Antonio's Gregg Popovich for Coach of the Year honors. "I began to get a lot of publicity and media attention," he told me. "Chuck called me and said, 'You're up too high. Be invisible. The players will resent you if they think you're trying to outdo them.'"

Another former Magic assistant, Tom Sterner, believed the secret lay in Chuck's personal sense of assurance. "Chuck Daly allowed his assistants to coach because he was confident in who he was," Tom said. "He made you feel appreciated and never showed any ego. Chuck knew what was important and what wasn't. He was not a micromanager, which made it enjoyable to work for him."

Chuck excelled at letting his players have their day in the sun. Former Detroit Pistons assistant coach Dick Versace recalls, "Chuck knew the best way to use his personnel and get the maximum out of them. Chuck was so bright, but you didn't realize it because he was so nice."

"Nothing ever fazed Chuck," remembers longtime sportscaster Dick Stockton, who worked with Chuck in his broadcasting years. "When we were doing a broadcast together, we'd finish the first quarter and Chuck would say, 'One down, three to go.' He never got too carried away with anything."

He kept his own ego under control, as his friend Evan "Big Cat" Williams, two-time long drive golf champion, testified. "Chuck got along with people so well. He was just a regular guy who never changed as success and fame came his way," Williams said. "Chuck never saw any reason to treat people differently or to make a big deal out of himself."

This aspect of Chuck's personality never changed. He was the same man from his days as a high school coach to the NBA. Dick Harter, who worked with Chuck at the University of Pennsylvania and later in Detroit, made this observation of Chuck's 1992 Olympic Dream Team role: "There were lots of egos in that group. "Chuck Daly's ego was never in play. All he did was see the good in everybody."

Julius Erving agrees with that assessment. "Chuck Daly was my dear friend," Dr. J told me. "He got along with everyone and always down-played his own ability."

Later in life, Chuck was a familiar figure at the Northwood University Seahawk games in West Palm Beach. Coach Rollie Massimino, who coached under Chuck at the University of Pennsylvania back in the early 1970s, has led the Northwood team for several years now. Over the decades, he and Chuck became close friends. "Here was this little NAIA school, he said, "and Chuck, a Hall of Fame coach, would come give them pep talks and watch their games."

The leadership principal here is that of possessing a servant's heart. It reminds me of the words of Rick Warren, author of *The Purpose Driven Life*, who opened that book with this now-classic line: "It's not about you." Long before *The Purpose Driven Life* came along, Chuck understood that. It's *always* about your players. It's always about *you*, not me. What can I do for *you*?

Moses spent forty years schlepping through the desert, walking in circles, but all the time leading the children of Israel to the Promised Land. At the end, Moses himself was denied entry. I'm sure he was disappointed, but he never forgot his job—to get the team across the goal line successfully. Lead and stay out of the spotlight.

CHUCKISM #19: YOU'VE GOT TO MAKE SURE THE GUYS WHO DON'T PLAY DON'T POISON THE GUYS WHO DO PLAY

"Chuck never played favorites. He knew how to treat guys and recognized they were all different and needed to be motivated individually," longtime NBA center Danny Schayes told me. Chuck spent time getting to know each player's personality. He knew which ones were the sparkplugs and which ones were likely to be circuit breakers.

A good coach starts his five best players and uses his bench players judiciously. The problem comes when the non-starters begin to stir up trouble behind the scenes and become "locker room lawyers." Chuck was a master at handling these complainers. He knew it was important to keep them from infecting the rest of the team.

Walt Disney is said to have observed that there were three kinds of people in life: the first group are the "well-poisoners," the nay-sayers, the negative people in your life. If you're having a personal parade, these folks are sure to bring the rain clouds with them. We all know our share of "well-poisoners."

Walt called the second kind "lawnmowers." These are people with no real ambition or vision—either for their own life or for yours. They get up every day and go to their jobs, but that's pretty much the end of the story. They might drive the floats in your parade, but there's no "oomph" in the engine. If you ask them for advice, they're likely to tell you to stay in your lane and don't go over the speed limit.

The third group are the "life enhancers." They are the ones who feed into the lives of others with rich, nutritious praise, advice, and encouragement. They pour their joy into other people. When you're feeling discouraged about the rainstorm that just opened up over your parade, the "life enhancer" brings back the sunshine.

Those grousers on the bench are quite often the "lawnmowers" of the team—average players who would never really be stars, but who could be useful at the right time. Chuck knew they could also easily become "well-poisoners." Dissatisfied that they're not getting playing time, they nitpick and find things to criticize.

Al McGuire, longtime basketball coach for Marquette University, had a great take on this topic. He'd say, "You can afford to have one donkey, but you can't have two—because they'll breed."

Are there people like this in your life? People who complain about even the best of products or services? People who never learned Thumper the bunny's lesson that "if you can't say something nice, don't say nuthin' at all"? Look for ways to surround yourself with "life enhancers"—and then go out and be one to someone else. Study the dynamics in your own groups and do what you can to keep the "well-poisoners" from winning the day.

CHUCKISM #20: COACHING BASKETBALL IS NOT ABOUT XS AND OS, BUT ABOUT DIVERSITY

In the eyes of the fans, Chuck Daly knew that only one thing mattered. Former Pistons executive Ron Campbell remembered this "ism" Chuck often used: "They are with you if you win or win big. Lose and they look at you cross-eyed. In the coaching profession, it all comes down to wins and losses." Chuck also knew that the NBA was an industry built around a core of talented people with the same struggles as the rest of society.

Annemarie Loflin was Chuck's former administrative assistant with the Orlando Magic. She told me, "Chuck was so perceptive. He was never wrong about people, or about situations. He told me, 'Coaching is not about the Xs and Os, but about managing diversity. Everyone is different, so you've got to study people and work with all of them differently. You've got to know which buttons to push.'"

Chuck valued diversity as a way to keep things fresh. "I always try to hire people for what I needed at that time," he would say. "I rarely hired someone I knew very well. I wanted new ideas. I always felt I needed, at different times, different personalities at different places."

"Chuck always believed the game was about the players and not him," said Tony Barone, Sr., who played for Chuck at Duke in the 1960s. "He never accepted any of the adulation that came his way because he knew the players dictated the game. He knew how to take advantage of their skills and play to their strengths."

A college baseball coach told me recently that to be a good leader you've got to be an electrician, constantly observing people to see how they're wired. You're studying how to configure or reconfigure that wiring to do the best job you can of motivating your people. Chuck Daly's greatest strength was his people skills. He was a student of the human spirit. And he was always working on those electrical skills. Maybe we should have put "Chuck the Electrician" on his Hall of Fame plaque.

"Chuck Daly had to deal with many, many different personalities on the Pistons," recalls NBA Hall of Famer Adrian Dantley. "His secret was not to let the little things bother him. He had a way of dealing with it that was very special."

As the Pistons' team physician for many years, Dr. Ben Paolucci saw this dynamic in action regularly. "Chuck Daly was a fine Xs and Os coach," he said, "but his real strength was dealing with people at all levels. Nobody did it better."

Chuck's longtime assistant and close confidant Brendan Suhr backs up Dr. Paolucci's sentiments. "Chuck knew that Xs and Os were not the most important part of basketball," Brendan told me. "It was the people who were playing. He had a great feel for his players and was aware the game was not about him."

Chuck kept his perspective fresh by seeking out friendships with people of all ages, like Gary Nicholas, producer and assistant director with TNT back when Chuck was doing NBA broadcasts. "Chuck and I became friends even though I was thirty years younger," Gary said. "It didn't matter, though, because he loved being around people. He was so accepting of everyone of all races and religions and was beloved by his players."

In 1992, Chuck's skills in pulling people and their strengths together for one heroic effort were really put to the test. He was tapped to coach the historic first Olympic Dream Team, made up of the best basketball players in the NBA. Suddenly he found himself in the locker room with stars like Charles Barkley, Larry Bird, Clyde Drexler, Patrick Ewing, Magic Johnson, Michael Jordan, Christian Laettner, Karl Malone, Chris Mullin, Scottie Pippin, David Robinson, and John Stockton. It was a Who's Who of the NBA.

In September 2009, this first-ever Dream Team was inducted into the NBA Hall of Fame. Chuck missed being part of it by four months. Clyde Drexler told USA Today, "[Chuck Daly] was the perfect personality to coach that team. We used to call him the Godfather. Nothing you did bothered Chuck Daly. He just wanted you to show up for practice and give it everything you had" (August 13, 2009, Page 3.0, "Drexler on Dream Team: Practice toughest").

Chuck had his own dream for this world-class competition, as I learned from broadcaster Don Shane. Don told me that before the 1992 Olympics, Chuck was asked what he personally wanted to accomplish. "He said, 'To never call a time out.' And he never did. They killed everybody," Don said.

Under Chuck, the American players scored more than 100 points in each of the eight games, with an overall victory margin of forty-three points. And zero timeouts called by Chuck Daly.

Chuck learned this technique of dealing with diversity early in his career. He credited Duke coach Vic Bubas with teaching him to "bite my tongue. You have to know when to talk to players and when to keep your peace. I learned to ask myself: Will this player benefit from what I say? Or will he just become less coachable? Sometimes I'd put my knuckles in my mouth or just look someplace else—anything to keep from saying what I was thinking" (from *Extreme Dreams Depend on Teams*, by Pat Williams and Jim Denney, Center Street 2009, pp. 209-210).

What great advice from Coach Daly. Learning to keep our cool could lead to stronger teams, and a much less contentious society.

CHUCKISM #21:
THEN GET IN EARLIER...BEAT ME IN

Bob Staak has had a long career coaching, both in college basketball and in the NBA. Bob worked as an assistant under Chuck Daly at the University of Pennsylvania in the early 1970s.

"When I went to work for Chuck," Bob told me, "I asked him what time should I be at work? He replied, 'Beat me in.' Later on I recall complaining that there wasn't enough time in the day to get everything done. Chuck's reply: 'Well, then get in earlier.'"

Bob Weinhauer was also one of Chuck's assistants at the University of Pennsylvania during that same time. "When we started at Penn it was summer time," he remembers. "We'd spend all day setting up recruiting schedules and going to summer league games and camps. We'd get back to the office at night and be back in again at 8 AM the next day. 'Chuck,' I said one day, 'there are only twenty-four hours in a day.' He replied, 'You can spend them all here.' It was never written down, but I felt I had to be in the office before he was and not leave to go home until after he did. In the end, you really didn't mind, because Chuck always made the day so comfortable for everyone around him."

My wife, Ruth, works for the FranklinCovey Company, teaching time management, organizational skills, and leadership principals, based on Stephen Covey's famous *The Seven Habits of Highly Effective People*. People ask me frequently, "How do you get everything done?" My answer is always, "I follow Ruth's instruction and maximize every minute of the day. Have a tightly organized schedule. Don't waste time. Stick closely to those areas of your life that are the most important."

As far as I know, Chuck Daly did not carry a Franklin Planner and I don't think he ever took Ruth's course. But long before Stephen Covey came along, these two "Chuckisms" carried the day:

"Beat me in."

"Then get in earlier."

Until a better approach comes along, give that one a whirl—and see what it does for adding more hours to your day.

CHUCKISM #22:
"EVERYTHING HAPPENS TO ME"

In 1940, the year Chuck Daly turned ten, songwriters Tom Adair and Matt Dennis sat down one day to reflect musically on life's more discouraging moments. The song that resulted was recorded by Frank Sinatra with the Tommy Dorsey orchestra. "Everything Happens to Me" became an instant hit. Apparently, many listeners could relate.

Chuck's close friend, broadcaster Jim Gray, who worked with Chuck on 76ers games in the early 1980s, told me, "If Chuck recited these words once, he said them a hundred times." Here's how they went:

"I make a date for golf—you can bet your life it rains.

I try to give a party, and the guy upstairs complains.

I guess I'll go through life just catchin' colds and missin' trains.

Everything happens to me."

Why would Chuck feel that way? After all, his late-blooming success in professional basketball had given his life a magical air. But one of his many nicknames was "The Prince of Pessimism"—and he had earned it.

So what was the appeal of these "woe is me" lyrics? I believe it's because Chuck was a realist. Like most of us, he was well acquainted with old Murphy—you know, the guy whose famous "law" turns up at all those inopportune times.

I think Chuck had known his share of plans that didn't work out, but he didn't let that stop him from making more plans. That's how we all need to be: hopeful but realistic. Every fall, we fully believe the Magic will capture the NBA crown that season. But the truth is, every team has talented players and excellent management. Not every team will take home the winner's trophy.

A contemporary way to say this is, "Reality bites." It often does, but don't let that stop you from dreaming. It didn't stop Chuck from leading the Pistons to two NBA titles or stepping into history as leader of the first-ever Olympic Dream Team. With a few victories like that in your life, you can handle occasional rain and complaining neighbors.

CHAPTER 4:
NEVER DO THAT

CHUCKISM #23:
NEVER TRUST HAPPINESS

We had good strong teams back when Chuck was an assistant with the 76ers. I remember saying, "Chuck, you've got to be happy with how the team is playing." He shot back firmly, "Never trust happiness."

What did he mean by that? Joe Dumars had heard him say it too. "Never let your guard down," is how Joe understood it. "You've got to prove yourself every day. Things may be good today, but that could completely change by tomorrow. Don't get too comfortable with success."

In the coaching business, you can have a ten-game winning streak, but as game eleven approaches, those last ten don't matter. I may have delivered twenty great speeches in a row, but number twenty-one is all the group I'm addressing next cares about. There's a tendency to get comfortable when things are going well. We think we've mastered the art. Chuck was great at cutting through that. You can't sit on your oars.

Jim Gray, Chuck's broadcasting friend, told me, "Chuck was never certain of his success and couldn't believe it was happening to him. He was sixty-years-old when these major league victories came his way. He thought it was all a mirage."

On the other hand, he could see disaster coming a mile off. Ron Campbell, who worked with Chuck in Detroit, told me, "He would say, 'It's going to be a fistfight.' It could be a tough game or a media interview or a negotiation. Chuck would announce in advance what was going to transpire."

Pistons trainer Mike Abdenour observed, "Chuck understood that this business will eat you alive if you're successful—and if you fail, it'll devour you. He believed it was important never to get too high or too low. He learned that winning is not as good as it seems and losing is not as bad as it seems. The sun will still come up the next day. Chuck was a man's man who respected the game at every level."

A related "Chuckism" here is "the wolves are always at the door." Detroit sportscaster Bernie Smilovitz of WDIV-TV remembers Chuck using this phrase often. "I think he was saying, 'When things are going good, they can always turn the other way," Bernie told me. "Always be prepared. Leave no stone unturned."

The great 49ers coach Bill Walsh summed up this philosophy recently in his brilliant leadership book *The Score Takes Care of Itself* (Portfolio, 2009). "While you're throwing a wolf out the back door, another is banging on the front door and two more are trying to crawl through the windows" (p. 9).

Never trust happiness—the wolves are always at the door. Be ready.

CHUCKISM #24:
NO ONE LOOKS BAD IN A BLUE SUIT

Every one of Chuck's friends will tell you the same story. He was the greatest window shopper of all time. He would go to men's clothing stores and wander through the racks, touching and feeling the material. But he'd never buy. "I can get this wholesale from my buddy in south Jersey. You never pay retail. There's always a deal," he would say.

Don Casey, former coach at Temple University, remembers, "We were in Minneapolis and must have visited nine men's clothing stores. Chuck was feeling the socks and checking the fabrics of the suits. And he was very restless—couldn't wait to get to the next store."

Even before Chuck became a wealthy head coach, he was a stickler for dressing to the *nth* degree. My first memory of him was as Vic Bubas's assistant in the mid-'60s. I thought, "Who is that good looking guy down on the bench, and where did he get those clothes?"

Hubie Brown remembers when Chuck was coaching at Duke and making $7500 a year. "Chuck had the ability to be the best dressed coach in the business with no money." Hubie said. "He knew how to schmooze with all the right clothing people."

On the day Chuck was named head coach at Penn, Don Casey was at the press conference. Don told me, "He was shimmering in a beautiful new suit. He wore gleaming alligator shoes. You could use them as a mirror. No one in the Big Five dressed like that. We had no style at all. But you know what? We changed and started trying to look like Chuck. He dressed up the entire Big Five."

"Chuck always wore a suit and tie because he represented the University of Pennsylvania," said Bob Weinhauer, Chuck's assistant there. "In the winter we would go out to lunch and there'd be slush on the ground. Chuck would never get a drop on his shoes or pant cuffs. We never could figure out how he did that."

When Chuck joined the 76ers in 1977, he took over our clothing duties. Billy Cunningham, our head coach, needed an enormous amount of work in the sartorial department—and I needed more. Chuck would never let you go seek out clothes without him. He made certain everything lined up, the ties and socks matched, and that you got the best price.

Bill Lyon, one of our local Philadelphia sports columnists back then, remembers, "Chuck was a real Dapper Dan. He wore those beautiful French cuffs with dazzling looking cuff links. I loved the way he'd shoot those cuffs out of his jacket. He made it look like an art form in itself. And then you'd see Chuck fingering the handmade tie to make sure the knot was perfect."

The folks in Detroit didn't know what was about to happen to them when Chuck Daly came to town in the early 1980s. Harry Hutt worked in marketing with the Pistons when Chuck was coach. He remembers that Chuck was always "reminding me of rule number one with a suit—always wear a silk pocket puff. None of us at the Pistons, including the players, ever *heard* of wearing a pocket puff until Chuck came along. It wasn't long before everyone had one to emulate the best-dressed coach."

Chuck wanted Hutt to step up his wardrobe and was ribbing him about his suit. Hutt pointed out to Chuck the salary difference between a marketing vice president and an NBA head coach, but Chuck would have none of it. So he took Harry shopping—to a place where Chuck had a "deal," of course. "He told me to pick out any suit in the store," Harry remembers. "I picked out a very fine suit that, of course, he approved of, and he said, 'It's on me.' I was flabbergasted that he did this. I still have that suit. I don't wear it anymore, but I can't stand to get rid of the suit Chuck gave me, all in the name of making me look better."

Chuck was also a fanatic on getting your hair *styled*—not cut. I was used to going down the street for my seven-dollar haircut, but Chuck soon eliminated that from my life. He introduced me to his hairstylist in Cherry Hill, New Jersey, Bobby Pileggi. I never returned to my neighborhood barber.

One year when I had a huge wedding anniversary, I had to come up with a fur coat on short notice. Chuck knew where to go. He sent me to the right guy at the right price.

Chuck Daly was more than just a sharp dresser, of course, but he knew that what we look like on the outside says a lot to others about the inner person. Memphis Grizzlies executive Andy Dolich told me, "Chuck always looked good on the outside, but he had the right stuff on the inside. That's what set him apart. He was not an empty suit."

After the cancer took hold, Chuck's sense of style was forced to give in a little to his sense of humor. Rollie Massimino recalls, "I saw Chuck every day the last three months of his life. He was losing his hair and he'd look at my bald head and say, 'If I had to look like you the rest of my life, I'd shoot myself.'"

Rollie remembers that Chuck hated to let things become useless. "Chuck loved clothes and wanted to always look his best," Rollie said. "And he wanted you to look your best. He had closets full of great threads. As he got sicker and sicker, he'd say to me, 'What a waste. What a waste.'"

At Chuck's NBA star-studded funeral, Rollie summed it up well: "He never paid retail for a closet filled with designer suits. He lived the good life, without ever spending very much. If he had known all these people were coming, he would have gotten out a brand new suit, made sure his shoes were shined and combed his hair to perfection" (http://www.nba.com/2009/news/features/05/13/daly.funeral/index.html).

At the end of the day we are initially judged by how we look. There are no days off, even on casual days. Chuck always looked like a million bucks. When you step out that door, you never know who's going to see you or whom you're going to meet. So *never* go out without looking your best. First impressions last.

Rick Mahorn, one of Chuck's "Bad Boy" Pistons, supplies a nice little "footnote" to this story: "Chuck taught me the importance of having a good pair of blue shoes to go with your blue suit." Make sure your first impression is both good and color-coordinated.

CHUCKISM #25: NEVER GET IN A FIGHT WITH A PERSON WHO BUYS INK BY THE BARREL

You can't whip the media. They always prevail and they *always* have the final word. You've got to work with them. I disobeyed this "Chuckism" early in my career, but I learned a painful lesson in the process.

In the early 1970s I was the young general manager of the Chicago Bulls. Bob Logan was a Bulls beat writer, and he was "beating up" on me—every day, it seemed. I really felt wronged, so I decided, *I'm going to get this fixed.* So I set up a meeting with Bob and Cooper Rollow, the *Chicago Tribune* sports editor, to vent and unload all the frustration I was feeling. I wanted this situation rectified and I would not settle for less.

I walked out of that meeting feeling very good about myself and thinking I had made great progress. But it was all just wishful thinking. Bob Logan was *not* happy that I had apparently showed him up in front of his boss. The ink attacks intensified. Never again have I thought about getting in a fight with any organization that buys ink by the barrel. They will win every time.

Chuck knew how important it was to build a positive reputation with the local press, any way he could do it. Coaching winning teams helped, but no one can do that every year. Still, he managed to gain enough respect that his name opened doors where it counted.

Don Casey remembers, "When I became the head coach at Temple, I replaced a legend in Harry Litwack. I had some rough sledding and was on shaky ground. Chuck was coaching at Penn then.

"One morning I picked up the *Philadelphia Inquirer* and there was a big story quoting Chuck that beating Temple was tougher than beating Princeton. (Princeton at the time was Penn's archrival under Pete Carril, a coaching wizard.) That one article may have saved my job and career. The authorities at Temple started to view me differently. You could make a case that Chuck Daly was one of the key people in my professional life."

Longtime *New York Times* columnist Harvey Araton observed, "There was a lot of humanity to Chuck Daly. He was always accessible to the media and would return your phone call promptly. He was a true sports gentleman as well as a fiercely competitive coach. That's a rare combination. All in all, Chuck was a classy guy to be around."

Chuck realized that most news gets old in a hurry. He'd learned not to panic over bad headlines. Ron Campbell recalls learning from Chuck, "If a negative event takes place, don't panic. It'll be gone by tomorrow. Then he'd say, 'Everything's a one-day story.'"

Sportscaster Dick Stockton nursed a little guilt for many years over some comments he'd made about Chuck, back when Chuck left Boston College to go to Penn. "I was doing sports commentaries on WBZ in Boston and I did a very critical piece on this and hit Chuck pretty hard," Dick remembers. "Many years later, I asked Chuck if he remembered that and wondered if he held it against me. Chuck said, 'No . . . it was a one-day story.'

Be respectful. Don't hold grudges. That's great advice for all of us.

CHUCKISM #26:
NEVER PUT A SADDLE ON A MUSTANG

If there was ever a season in which Chuck Daly learned to respect the intense rivalry between top players, it was during the 1992 Olympic Dream Team competition.

He was coaching the best players in the world on a huge international stage. And Chuck was trying to get them to cooperate and play like a team, a feat that was like trying to saddle a mustang.

Veteran NBA coach Lenny Wilkens was one of Chuck's assistants on that history-making team. "Chuck worried about everything," Lenny recalls. "We won the Tournament of the Americas. Then we went on to Nice, France and whipped France. Chuck Daly wasn't pleased with our practices, so he set up a scrimmage for the ages. Magic Johnson's team was killing Michael Jordan's team. Then Magic gets on MJ. Clyde Drexler gets fired up. MJ goes nuts. It was unbelievable. Chuck had to stop the practice it was so intense."

NBA coach-turned broadcaster P. J. Carlesimo also assisted Chuck with the Dream Team. He concluded, "As the Olympic coach, Chuck managed those great personalities like no one else could have imagined. This was the first true gathering of the modern athlete and Chuck was great at getting his points across in a non-confrontational way."

Like a skilled horse-whisperer, Chuck studied his players on every team he coached. "Chuck was uncanny with his insights into people and what made them tick," observed Bill Raftery, broadcaster for the New Jersey Nets. "For example, in the pre-practice stretching routine, he'd say, 'Did you see who was stretching with so and so?' That kind of stuff just fascinated him."

"Chuck came up to me one day after I'd worked with Dennis Rodman and said, 'Don't put a saddle on a mustang,'" remembers Brendan Malone. "He was telling me he didn't want Dennis thinking too much. All he wanted Dennis to do was defend, rebound, and play free like a mustang. If ever there was a mustang that played in the NBA, it was Dennis. Chuck was right again. He knew his players strengths and weaknesses."

Hubie Brown followed Chuck's career closely from the day they'd worked as assistants with Vic Bubas. He believed Chuck was selected as Dream Team coach for these six reasons:

- He had the ability to listen.

- He could communicate with superstars.

- He had the perfect image and resume.

- He had the proper communication skills to deal individually with the greatest players ever. Those players could overpower most coaches.

- Chuck golfed with them. He had the knack of staying aloof from them but still being close.

- He was always in charge.

In the now-classic business book *Good to Great* (HarperBusiness, 2001), author Jim Collins talks at length about the importance of having "the right people on the bus." Chuck Daly could have been the living illustration for that principle. As the "bus driver," he took pains to get to know his players' strengths and weaknesses, to not only get the right people on the bus, but sitting in the right seats as well.

Because he'd spent years perfecting that management style, by the time the Dream Team arrived in Barcelona, Chuck was well acquainted with mustang herding. Not only was the team undefeated, but the closest score in any of the games was the final, which the Dream Team won 117-85.

Chuck aptly said of his eventually disciplined wild horses, "You will see a team of professionals in the Olympics again, but I don't think you'll see another team quite like this. This was a majestic team."

In the end, Chuck realized that while it's not smart to put saddles on mustangs—you can learn to drive them home as a team.

CHAPTER 5:
ALWAYS Do This

CHUCKISM #27:
PRACTICE THE MIDNIGHT RULE

Chuck would tell you this was an old Irish philosophy, and here's how it worked:

The game was usually over by about 9:30 PM. If you won, everybody was happy. The coaches would go out to eat and celebrate. If you lost, everybody was miserable. They would cry about their fates and how unfair it was, how the game was "stolen," or how "the refs killed us."

But at 12 midnight, all celebration or commiserating had to end. At 12:01 AM, it was time to focus on the next day. In a way, I suppose it was something like the story of Cinderella, whose glass slipper disappeared and golden coach reverted to a pumpkin at midnight. The party's over. Win or lose, it's time to get back to real life.

Paul Silas, Chuck's former assistant with the New Jersey Nets, told me, "Chuck taught me never to say anything to the players after the game because everyone is too emotional. Wait 'til the next day when you are all calmed down. That was a coaching principle I used when I became a head coach."

"Chuck never dwelt on wins and losses after a game," said Derrick Coleman, who started his career playing for Chuck with the New Jersey Nets. "He never got too high or too low, either way. He always reminded us, 'We've got another game to play.'"

Longtime New Jersey Nets broadcaster Bill Raftery worked with Chuck Daly when he coached that team from 1992 to 1994. Bill said, "The game would be over and we'd get on a plane to fly to the next game. En route, Chuck would always put in a tape of the next opponent, not the one we had just played that night."

Brendan Suhr worked with Chuck during the Pistons back-to-back championship seasons. He recalls hearing Chuck say often, "'Never look back!' Chuck believed that was why they make windshields bigger than rearview mirrors."

"In the 1990 Eastern Conference finals, we were playing the Bulls in game seven at home, trying for our second championship," Suhr remembers. "We'd been whipped in game six in Chicago on a Friday, and now we had the Bulls on Sunday afternoon. Brendan Malone and I had worked all weekend to get a video ready to show the team before the game. We were about to start when Chuck walked in and yelled, 'We're the defending NBA champs and I don't care about the last game!' He threw the tape we had prepared up against a wall, smashing it into a million pieces. We went out and killed the Bulls by about 20—and went on to win that second title. Chuck knew how to do it."

Dan Hauser, the Detroit Pistons Executive Vice President, said, "Chuck taught me not to carry yesterday's baggage into today. I don't have it mastered yet, but I'm still working at it." And so should we all.

We have three blocks of time to deal with in our lives:

- The first is *yesterday*. Learn from it. Grow from your past. But don't pitch a tent in yesterday. The past is meant to be a springboard—not a hammock.

- *Tomorrow* isn't here yet. There's nothing wrong with looking to the future, but so many of us live in a future that never materializes. We waste a lot of time by doing this.

- Focus on the next twenty-four hours—*today*.

As I'm getting older, I find I can't handle anymore than just one day at a time. If I look at next week's schedule, it overwhelms me. Every hour in my Franklin Planner is spoken for—most of the time! So I'm working hard at honoring Chuck and always practicing the midnight rule. I think Cinderella figured that out too.

CHUCKISM #28:
TAKE THE HIGH ROAD

The finish to Chuck's career in Detroit was not pleasant for him. He knew going in it would be his last year there. His replacement was already waiting in the wings. It was a difficult situation.

Detroit Pistons President Tom Wilson recalls, "Chuck coached through that season as the Bulls were launching their dynasty with Michael Jordan. Just before Chuck's farewell press conference, he said to me privately, 'Always take the high road.' And that's what Chuck did publicly, no matter what he felt privately. He told me, 'When your time comes it's important to leave the right way. The world will still keep going around.' Chuck advised all of us to do that.

"Vinnie Johnson was the first key Pistons' player to be traded after the run of titles, and he was really angry about it," Tom continued. "Vinnie wanted to go out with fire and venom, but Chuck took him out to dinner and told him to 'take the high road.' At his final press conference, Vinnie did that, and went out on a high note. Chuck told him, 'You have a lot of friends in Detroit and you'll end up coming back here.' That's exactly what happened. Vinnie has had huge success in the automotive parts industry and remains a highly-regarded citizen of the Detroit community."

Matt Guokas, former Philadelphia 76ers and Orlando Magic head coach, remembers, "Chuck taught me that you could have a confrontation every day, but why go there? They generally don't solve things, so don't end the day on a down note with anyone. Stay focused on what goes on between the lines."

Chuck taught us all that laying your ego down over the small things makes it second nature when the heat is on. His close friend Matt Dobek, longtime media relations director for the Pistons, remembers Chuck using this "Chuckism" repeatedly during that final year in Detroit: "I'm just gonna take the high road." Chuck had determined in advance to handle everything with dignity and class.

I remember once with the 76ers when I needed Chuck's advice. The owner had reneged in a situation I'd been handling and redid what I had done. I was not happy. In fact, I was downright upset. Chuck pulled me aside and used that phrase: "Pat," he said to me, "take the high road."

In so many situations, you can explode and foolishly pop off, only to regret it later. You can become obsessed, paranoid, have a false sense of pride, and end up stomping self-righteously down the low road—most often alone. That's where you get destroyed.

In the end, Chuck refused to let anything take him down—not even death itself. Veteran beat writer Phil Jasner told me, "When Chuck was sick in the hospital in March, 2009, Villanova was doing well in the NCAA tournament. Chuck was following their run on television. One day some coaching friends were visiting Chuck at the hospital and Chuck had drawn up a special play for Villanova coach Jay Wright. Chuck said, 'Give this to Jay. It always works for me.'"

When I think of the high road, I think of Chuck Daly and these two key words: class and dignity. They will win out every time.

CHUCKISM #29: YOU'D BETTER KNOW WHERE YOUR NEXT JOB IS COMING FROM

Chuck Daly took nothing for granted. Not even his next job. He encouraged his players to live like that too. You never know when you'll be traded or cut from the roster, he would tell them. Today's hero becomes tomorrow's zero in a hurry. "Chuck was a very smart coach and decent guy," recalls best-selling author Mitch Albom, who spent many years as a sportswriter and broadcaster in Detroit. "Chuck got it regarding pro sports: they hire you to fire you." So you've got to be prepared. And you've got to have a keen sense of timing.

Chuck loved to tell the story of his first "dream" trip to an NCAA championship, back in 1963. He was coaching high school basketball in Pennsylvania at the time and had a chance to see the Final Four games in Louisville, Kentucky. He sat in the back row of the upper balcony and had the "worst seat in the house," he said, after purchasing a scalped ticket. Shortly after the tournament, he applied for an open position as Vic Bubas's assistant at Duke—and was stunned when he got the job. That year, 1964, the Duke team made it to the Final Four. They were defeated by John Wooden's UCLA Bruins—who were just getting started on ten championships seasons—but what a career move it had been for Chuck. Exactly one year after sitting in the last row of the building, he sat on the bench next to Coach Bubas. "I went from the worst seat in the house to the best!" he wrote. "If it can happen to me, it can happen to anyone" (*Chicken Soup for the Soul: Inside Basketball: 101 Great Hoop Stories from Players, Coaches and Fans*, Chicken Soup for the Soul Publishers, 2009).

Former Pistons general manager Jack McCloskey knew he was taking a chance when he brought Chuck to Detroit. "Chuck had a very short and unsuccessful tour as the Cleveland Cavaliers' coach," Jack said, "and I took a lot of criticism when I hired him as head coach. But I had known Chuck when he was coaching at Penn and knew he was a good basketball man. The main thing I liked about Chuck was he had a good temperament for our team. We had a bunch of really strong personalities and I knew Chuck could handle those tough situations in the right way."

Pistons guard Joe Dumars remembers a related "Chuckism": "They can replace you in this business."

"In other words," Joe added, "don't get a big head. You're always vulnerable. You're only as good as your last win."

Don Shane, a veteran Detroit sports announcer, observed, "Chuck had the gift of taking twelve basketball egos and molding them together to win championships. His main goal was not to get in their way as superb athletes so they could perform to their maximum. I once asked him when he'd know it was time to go. He said, 'When they stop listening to me.'"

Late in life, long after Chuck had mastered all the jobs he'd ever wanted, came one last opportunity. NBA executive Harry Hutt remembers the time when Chuck, the Depression-era boy from a poor coal-mining town, turned down a lot of money and a final shot at NBA glory. It was 2002, and Chuck was retired. Harry was working for the Portland Trailblazers and they were in desperate need of a new coach.

"Trailblazer president Bob Whitsitt asked me about Chuck," Harry told me. "Would he give it another go? I said I would find out. So I called Chuck that night and we talked for about a half hour. He was interested—I think the coal mining heritage of his was intrigued by having a billionaire like Paul Allen as an owner."

But Chuck needed some time to think it over. Harry was surprised when Chuck turned it down a few days later. The timing was all wrong, he said. His wife, Terry, had recently suffered a stroke. She was recovering well, but Chuck would not ask her to move, nor would he leave her 3,000 miles behind.

"The consummate coach, the NBA master, had one more chance with a powerful team owned by a billionaire who didn't meddle," Hutt observed. "What more could Chuck ask for? There was a lot of substance and sensitivity underneath all the flash and dash." Chuck chose his lifetime partner over the NBA.

It's important to know your priorities. What do you really want to do, and what are you willing to compromise in order to get there? What are the deal-breakers for you? If you figure those things out in advance, you can save yourself a lot of frustration.

Chuckism #30:
Let's go! Let's go!

Chuck Daly was *not* patient. If anything was taking too long, in his estimation, you'd inevitably hear him shout out, "Let's go, let's GO!"

Kim Bohuny was working in the NBA offices when Chuck and the Dream Team players were prepping for the 1992 Olympics. She told me the story of their stop in Monaco and their audience with Prince Rainier.

On this day, the Prince was not as punctual as Chuck would have preferred, and after a few minutes (literally) his familiar restless, panther-like prowl kicked in. Back and forth he paced. "When I went to the White House," he complained, "the president saw me right away! He didn't make me wait."

John Gabriel, who was the Orlando Magic's general manager when Chuck was signed, hammered out what was one of the largest coaching contracts in NBA history. On the day of the signing, John was to drive to Chuck's home in south Florida. He had a few hiccups getting started and was running late, but called Chuck to let him know. Chuck's response on that day of the biggest deal of his life: "Let's go, let's GO!"

Chuck saw no need for long drawn out practice sessions, either. Nick Anderson spent thirteen years in the NBA before retiring in 2002, most of them with the Orlando Magic. Anderson recalls, "He'd laugh and joke with you. He'd say to us, 'Why practice for two and a-half hours when you can get it done in an hour.' One day he came to practice and said, 'It's eleven o'clock. I've got a tee time at noon.'"

Former teammate Darrell Armstrong agrees with Anderson, adding, "Chuck would come to the gym, get practice done and move on. He was always prepared and did everything the right way."

There were a few variations on this "Chuckism":

"I understand—got it in ten seconds; I don't need the whole alphabet." If you had something to say to Chuck, you'd better be ready to deliver it in the *Reader's Digest* condensed version. Leave your long-winded stories for your mother.

And then there was, "If you don't know already, I can't explain it." Chuck was not a man for repeating things. If the look on your face said, "I don't get it"—it was too bad. You were on your own.

This is not to negate Chuck's role as teacher—not at all. He did have a talent—even a love—for storytelling. Neil Funk was a longtime NBA broadcaster in Philadelphia who worked with Chuck one year between coaching stints, when Chuck was doing color analysis. "As a broadcaster Chuck could take a complex basketball situation and explain it in a simple way to make the average fan understand," Neil said. "He told listeners how and why things occurred."

But at his core, Chuck was a doer. He taught by showing rather than telling. It's a great leadership habit to develop.

Chuckism #31: You've got to go through the process. Keep moving forward

Chuck was always willing to do whatever it took to reach his goal. He "personified the process," said Don Casey, who coached at both the college and professional level. Casey continued, "That's what Chuck did. He coached in high school and then as a college freshman coach, a college assistant, a college head coach, an NBA assistant, an NBA head coach. Chuck hit every base, including the Olympics. His philosophy was to go out and pay your dues, go to the clinics, build a network of contacts, work hard. When he died, one newspaper headline read 'Dues-Paying Coach Chuck Daly Dead at 78.'"

Chuck knew you don't get anywhere sitting still. He was known for saying, "You've got to keep moving forward." "Keep building your résumé," Casey added. "Don't get satisfied, don't be stagnant, keep stretching yourself."

Walt Disney once said of his operation, "Around here . . . we don't look backwards for very long. We keep moving forward, opening up new doors and doing new things, because we're curious . . . and curiosity keeps leading us down new paths."

Daly and Disney were in vastly different businesses, but both men specialized in developing their talent and then doing what they did best. Set the bar high in your own life. Go through the process. Keep moving forward.

CHUCKISM #32:
TRUST ME

When Chuck knew he was absolutely right about a thing—when he knew he had the answer—there was simply no need to prolong the discussion. When Chuck said those two words, "Trust me," it was time to turn out the lights and go home.

Joe Dumars, now a Pistons executive, said, "Chuck never lost the human element of coaching. As a result, people trusted him. None of his players were ever just a piece of meat to him. Chuck understood that if you make your people feel good about themselves, they will follow you. He was a great coach technically, but there has never been a coach with a better human spirit."

People trust you when they can relate to you, when they sense you have danced the court in their shoes. Chuck knew his team had to trust him or there would be no winning seasons.

Even more critical than the coach/player trust is the relationship between a parent and a child. Former Detroit sports writer Charlie Vincent told me this great story: "It was the second week of May 1987, and the Pistons were in the second round of the NBA playoffs. Chuck was still trying to establish himself and the franchise after losing in the first round of playoffs to the Hawks the year before. This season, the Pistons had beaten Washington in the first round, then split two games in Atlanta on May 3 and 5, losing the second by thirteen points. Games three and four were scheduled at the Silverdome on May 8 and 10."

Somewhere in the midst of all this excitement, came his daughter Cydney's graduation day from Penn State University in State College, Pennsylvania. Because of the playoffs, she'd reluctantly accepted that her dad would not be there.

Cydney told Charlie, "I was running around my apartment, late like I always am, when the doorbell rang. When I answered it, there stood Dad with this big bunch of balloons in his hand. He had chartered a private plane and asked the pilot to wait through the ceremony. Then he flew back to Detroit."

The Pistons went on to the finals that season but lost out to the Celtics for the NBA crown. Still, the team did very well and Chuck's reputation as a head coach was established. More importantly, his standing as a dad had gone up at least a hundred points in Cydney's eyes.

Scott Crites, founder of a business organization that often asked Chuck to speak, remembers, "On several occasions, we had booked Chuck when his wife, Terry, was struggling with some health issues. I was always impressed with Chuck's commitment to her. He was talking to me constantly about Terry and seemed so loyal to her. That left a real impression on me and served as a checkpoint for my marriage."

The trust people had in Chuck extended to those associated with him. Kathy Collins, wife of former four-time NBA All-Star Doug Collins, told me, "I had a great respect for Terry Daly. She taught me how to be a coach's wife . . . how to handle myself and act with dignity."

Establishing trust is not easy. If you utter those two words, "Trust me," you'd better make sure you've earned the right. Chuck Daly did every day.

CHUCKISM #33:
GET PAST MAD

During a lengthy conversation with Chuck's daughter, Cydney, she told me about some conversations with her father. "I would be upset or angry about some situation," she told me, "and I'd say to my dad, 'I'm so mad about what happened here' or 'I'm mad about what they did to me.' And my dad would say, 'Honey, get past mad.'"

"What did he mean, Cydney?" I asked.

"Move on," she said. "Get over it. Don't get your ulcers whipped into a frenzy. If you're churning yourself up over this situation, the other person probably doesn't even remember it, and you're taking a toll on your own mental and physical health."

Chuck was known throughout the league as a man who simply did not boil over. Wayne Embry, a former player and longtime NBA executive, told me, "Chuck once explained to me that it does no good to confront players during a game when you are angry. Take a walk down the beach, get some water, sit down and coach. Never confront them and get them steamed at you. You need these guys to play for you."

If team members resent their leader, they will not perform for him. When the heat is on, they will simply melt.

More than once, Chuck told his coaches, players, and family members to "get past mad." He well understood the damage unchecked anger often unleashes. Once it's out there, it's awfully hard to rein it back in.

Bob Zuffelato, an NBA veteran and former assistant coach with Chuck, remembers the time Chuck told him to "get past mad." One day he was feeling pretty hot under the collar about several things and went to Chuck's office to vent. Bob recalls, "Chuck put his hand up and said, 'Wait a minute. Do you want to be a head coach?' I nodded, 'Yes.' 'You see the problems you've got now?' Chuck pointed out. 'As a head coach, you can multiply them by ten.'"

Life is rarely fair. Every day brings a fresh crop of problems. You can't explode every time someone gets in your face. "Get past mad." That's good advice for all of us.

CHAPTER 6:
THAT'S LIFE

CHUCKISM #34:
I'M A PRODUCT OF THE GREAT DEPRESSION

As the members of what author Tom Brokaw called "The Greatest Generation" begin to thin out, there are fewer and fewer people who remember what it was like when America suffered through the Great Depression of the 1930s. Even though Chuck was just a boy during that dark decade, he never forgot its lessons in thrift. They shaped his life. Even after attaining success as an NBA coach, he lived frugally.

Veteran broadcaster Neil Funk remembers that Chuck would often advise him, "'Get a receipt. Receipts are like cash.' You can give it to your taxman. I'd buy a thirty-nine cent candy bar and Chuck would say, 'Did you save the receipt?'"

Harry Hutt, who worked in the Detroit Pistons front office in the late 1980s, told me, "One day during the 1987-88 season, Chuck strolled, unannounced, into my office at the Silverdome. This was not unusual. He would do this every now and then, usually just hobnobbing with people in the front office, but always on the lookout for some freebie—a restaurant gift certificate, a watch, or anything that struck his fancy. I would kid him about how with his coaching paycheck he surely didn't need a free dinner certificate. Chuck would just smile unashamedly and say, 'When you're from the Pennsylvania coal mine country, growing up like I did, you never have enough, no matter how much money you make.' And then he would flash that million dollar smile and charm the gift certificate out of your desk."

Chuck never felt comfortable with luxuries most of us would take for granted. Over the years, rock-ribbed fiscal discipline guided his decisions and became his trademark. When the Magic made him coach in 1997, we convinced him to move into an upscale neighborhood in town. Even though we covered his moving expenses, uber-frugal Chuck rented a U-Haul and had his assistant coaches help him with the boxes.

Golfer Evan "Big Cat" Williams remembers the time Chuck told him, "I was really tempted last night. I went back to the hotel after the game and there were two Godiva chocolates on the pillow. I'd given up chocolate for lent and I wanted those two so badly. But I didn't do it. It just wasn't worth it."

An avid golfer, Chuck simply could not get used to living a country club lifestyle. Isiah Thomas remarked, "If you ever looked in his garage, you'd find about 900 golf clubs, every one he ever owned," Thomas said. "He couldn't bear the thought of throwing out the old ones. He always wondered if this would last" (http://nba.fanhouse.com/2009/05/13/bad-boys-return-to-honor-chuck-daly/).

My mother was fifteen when the stock market crashed back in 1929, so she lived through the Great Depression. It was over by the time I came along, but I can still hear her voice saying, "Save your money!" "We can't afford that." "Don't spend what you don't have."

"Put it in your savings bank." "Don't do anything to ruin your credit." If Mom's advice had been broadcast worldwide, we might have avoided the entire financial crisis that began showing its fangs in 2008.

Here's another expression undoubtedly born of Chuck's Great Depression childhood: "Hit the lottery! Twenty dollars won't change my life; $30,000,000 will." Chuck understood the value of a dollar.

CHUCKISM #35:
WHAT DO YOU DO BEST?

This story has a couple of versions. I'm sure Isiah Thomas tells it a little differently, but here is Chuck's view: In the late 1980s and early '90s, the Pistons were a dominant team. But they struggled from time to time. During one of those periods, Chuck was upset and went after his captain, Isiah Thomas, in a rather heated exchange:

Chuck: "Isiah, what is it you do best?"

Isiah: "Lead, Coach."

Chuck: "Well then, lead!"

Chuck was challenging his leader to lead.

In our society today, we desperately need men and women in leadership positions who will step up and start leading. What are the qualities of great leaders? I believe they are these:

1. **Vision** – The ability to see the future before it gets here. There are two kinds of people in the world: realists and visionaries. Realists know where they're going; visionaries have already been there.

2. **Communication** – Leadership gravitates to the people who can talk, who can stand up and say what they think.

3. **People skills** - Eddie Robinson, former football coach at Grambling State University, said, "You've got to coach every player as if he were going to marry your daughter. You can't coach 'em if you don't love 'em." Chuck's longtime friend Don Magnuson noted, "Chuck Daly's greatest coaching strength was his ability to relate to his players. They loved him for it." Bill Lyon, Philadelphia sports columnist, found Chuck to be "a very engaging guy. As a reporter, there were a lot worse ways to spend an hour than talking hoops with Chuck."

4. **Character** – Old-fashioned values still count in leadership: honesty, integrity, work ethic, humility, responsibility, perseverence, and courage. As leadership expert John Maxwell says, "You can only go as high as your character will allow you."

5. **Competence** – Leaders are good at what they do. They're often born with certain gifts, but great leaders are always working to improve and enhance their leadership capabilities. My friend Ernie Accorsi, longtime NFL executive, told me about watching championship quarterback Johnny Unitas walk off the Baltimore Colts team bus when they were on the road. Something about Johnny U's presence made you

feel the team was in good hands. Chuck Daly had that same aura. Be someone whose competence inspires confidence.

6. **Boldness** – Chuck said to Isiah Thomas, "You've got to step up and lead." So do you. Don't be afraid to make decisions.

7. **Serving heart** – The world needs more leaders whose lives are about helping other people and doing all you can to enhance their future.

Study these characteristics. Work at them. Knead them into your own life until they become part of your personal DNA. Then lead on.

CHUCKISM #36:
CONSEQUENCE OF ACTION

I was having lunch one day with Chuck's daughter, Cydney, in Orlando, where she lives with her two children. She told me her story of growing up around the Pistons in the 1980s. One day, she said, she was talking with some of the players and threw out the phrase, "consequence of action." The players turned in astonishment and said, "Your dad says that to you too?"

"I grew up with those three words pounding in my brain," Cydney recalled. "Every action you take has consequences and you have to live with them." As nineteenth century author Robert Louis Stevenson wrote, "Everybody, soon or late, sits down to a banquet of consequences."

One day, Magic team captain Derek Harper learned what this phrase meant. "On the first road trip of the season," recalls Chuck's then-assistant coach Eric Musselman, "we had a 3 PM departure. Derek was running late and phoned the trainer with the news that he was on his way. It was two minutes of three when Chuck said to the flight attendant, 'What time does the itinerary say?' 'Three o'clock,' she said. Chuck said, 'Wheels up at three. We're out of here.' Then Chuck looked at me and winked and said, 'That's a tough call, but one that's gotta be made.'" You might say Harper suffered a consequence of inaction.

Cydney Daly still remembers the same thing happening to her when she was in high school. The 76ers had a Sunday afternoon playoff game at the Spectrum in Philadelphia. Cydney recalls, "I was being a typical teenage girl and taking too long getting my hair ready. Dad said we were leaving in five minutes, and I didn't appear in time. Just as I got to the door, Dad and Mom were pulling out of the driveway, and off they went to the game. I ended up watching the game at home on TV with the best looking hair you've ever seen. I'll never forget that day—and I was never late for my father again."

Every decision has a consequence. Therefore, the better your decisions, the better the consequences. Over the course of a lifetime, that can mean a much more fulfilling and productive life. If you're busy dealing with all the fires of poor decisions, you can't move aggressively forward to do those things that advance your career and your success.

Here's a great little rule of thumb from one of my favorite authors, Andy Stanley. Every time you have a decision to make, he says, ask yourself the best question ever: "In light of my past experiences and my future hopes and dreams, what is the wise thing to do?" If you did that every time, Andy points out, think of all the regret you wouldn't have and all the remorse that wouldn't be there.

No matter your station in life, no matter how far you are down the road, it's never too late to start asking the best question ever. Then you'll hear Chuck's words pounding in your brain, just as Cydney does: "Consequence of action."

CHUCKISM #37:
BEYOND BELIEF...BEYOND BEYOND

Brendan Suhr remembers Chuck using this phrase often when something struck him as amazing or better than great. He so enjoyed the stage performance of *Phantom of the Opera*, for example, that he came back with this one line review: "Beyond belief!"

Praise is sadly lacking in our society today—or at least it is misdirected. We praise people for achievements that are far from being "beyond belief" and fail to praise those who really have earned it.

Chuck knew encouragement is a key ingredient in developing and motivating your team. "Shout praise and whisper criticism," he was known for saying.

Praise builds confidence—in your children, your co-workers, and your life team members. Each one of us is "beyond belief" at times. Let's make sure we note those times that are, as Chuck Daly might say when really exhilarated, "beyond beyond."

CHUCKISM #38: YOU DON'T REALLY KNOW WHO YOU ARE UNTIL YOU'RE AT LEAST THIRTY-FIVE

Chuck was a firm believer in the role of maturity in our lives. That's a hard word in a society where we want everything now. Maturity requires one special ingredient: t-i-m-e.

My friend Jay Strack, founder of Student Leadership University in Orlando, describes maturity as the moment when the child has decided to sit down permanently and the young adult has decided to stand up permanently.

It's important for young people to experiment and be exposed to a lot of different interests. Parents—I recommend that with your children. When the Bible says, "Train up your child in the way he should go," this is what it's talking about. Your job is to help them figure out what it is they're shaped to do.

By the time you're thirty-five, you need to have your life on track. You'll have your college degree—and maybe a graduate degree or two. You may be married by this time, with a young family. You'll undoubtedly have made a big mistake or two and discovered you can survive it. It's time now for your sense of where you're headed to be solid.

If you're not yet thirty-five—be patient with yourself. Take time to get to know your own preferences and the non-negotiables you won't compromise. Build and develop your character as much as you can through classes and books. Sit down and write out what you believe. When you know who you are, you'll save yourself a lot of frustration down the road.

A lot of Chuck's success may have come later in life, but by the time he was thirty-five he had no doubts as to his personal goals. He was a basketball coach. He was a man of principle who always put his family first. He was a loyal friend and a man who led by example.

CHUCKISM #39: YOUTH MUST BE SERVED— YOU DON'T STAY ON TOP FOREVER

As he got older, Chuck understood the stigma of "looking old" in a culture that wants it all—experience and youthful looks all in the same package. He knew he'd come into the NBA a little later than most coaches and it worried him. So he worked hard at not looking old.

Harry Hutt remembers the day Chuck began giving him a hard time over the gray creeping into his sideburns. "You need to put a little *stuff* on you," Chuck said. "What are you talking about?" Hutt replied, "What *stuff*? And put it where?" Chuck smiled. "You need a little *stuff*, a little color in your sideburns. I see a couple of gray hairs there."

"'Well, yeah," Hutt agreed. "I do have a couple gray hairs. I'm not twenty-nine anymore. But what's the big deal?"

Chuck leveled a gaze and said, "Don't ever forget—this is a young man's game. Put some *stuff* on your sideburns.'

"I thought about it after he left my office," Hutt said. "It wasn't just the clothes with Chuck but it was also how he 'looked' to people, and 'looking' young was not so much about being vain as it was making sure he never 'looked' too 'old' to be an NBA coach."

Wendy Schayes, wife of longtime NBA center Danny Schayes, remembers the day Chuck "showed me a photo of Pat Riley out in a boat with his hair blowing freely in the wind. Chuck was so excited and said, 'See—his hair is completely gray!' Pat knew nothing about it, but Chuck was competitive with him over gray hair."

There comes a time when we must move over and make way for the next generation. That doesn't mean, however, that there is not still life left in us old "clunkers." No need to crush us down for scrap metal just yet. I believe that "you're only as old as you feel."

"The word I think of with Chuck Daly is vibrant," said Harvey Araton, who covered Daly and his teams frequently in his New York *Times* NBA columns. "He looked vibrant, exuded vibrancy in his movements and produced results that were vibrant—and he always looked ten years younger than he was!" Chuck was eternally young, both in looks and in attitude.

I'm still feeling pretty chipper—how about you? Chuck taught us all how to live fully to the last minute—and how to do it looking and feeling young.

Chuckism #40:
It is what it is

On its surface, that statement seems kind of obvious once you hear it—but like so many profound statements, it's not always obvious *until* you analyze it. And Chuck said it a lot when the going wasn't going so well.

Duke University head basketball coach Mike Krzyzewski remembers, "In all situations where someone might look at a problem and get worried or anxious, Chuck's great line was, 'It is what it is' to relieve tension. It grounded everyone, and we were able to deal with whatever situation was facing us. It was a brilliant way of doing things. I use that line all the time."

During the Magic's 2009 NBA championship competition with the Los Angeles Lakers, I found myself recalling this line a lot. Our team played well. After all, we'd made it to the Finals, beating out the Cleveland Cavaliers and the dazzling LeBron James to get there. We had a lot going for us and had many good reasons to be proud. But what those Lakers had was downright amazing. Kobe, Odom, Gasol— they all played truly over-the-top basketball in that series. Game after knuckle-chewing game, I found myself concluding, "It is what it is." When the series ended with the Lakers taking yet another well-deserved NBA title back to Los Angeles, well—it was what it was.

Life is full of tense moments, times when we're not sure what the outcome will be. When we find ourselves in one, we really have two choices: we can work our knickers into a knot with worry and manipulative tactics—or we can say with Chuck Daly, "It is what it is," and let the chips fall where they may. In the end, that's how it will turn out anyhow. So why not get there without the wrinkled knickers?

When Chuck was a young man, songstress Doris Day had a popular tune on everyone's lips. It's refrain declared, "Que sera, sera. Whatever will be will be. The future's not mine to see. Que sera, sera." Somehow I can picture him riding around in a red 1950s convertible, top down, breeze blowing through his perfectly styled hair, singing along with Doris.

So many young people today are impatient for the results, frustrated when things don't come out their way. I've seen this in the lives of my own adult children. Chuck would tell you to do all you can to prepare, but realize that at some point, "it is what it is." Release the outcome with a sweet serenade of "Que sera, sera!" Say to the Lord, "Your will be done." Let it go. Let it be.

CHAPTER 7:
ATTITUDE IS EVERYTHING

CHUCKISM #41:
A PESSIMIST IS AN OPTIMIST WITH EXPERIENCE

Along the way Chuck had acquired the nickname "The Prince of Pessimism." If you asked him a question about the season or an upcoming game, Chuck always seemed worried. Ron Campbell, who knew Chuck in Detroit, remembers, "When the NBA schedule would come out in July, Chuck Daly's first thought was, 'We're going 0-82. There's not a win here.'" Chuck was known for many things, but being positive was not one of them.

He'd be so concerned and uneasy, you'd come away thinking things must be really bad. But if you called him "The Prince of Pessimism" to his face, he'd reply, "No! A pessimist is just an optimist with experience."

"I can't get caught up in all the hoopla and well wishes," Chuck would say. "If I hope to keep my objective glasses on, I've got to take the rosy ones off."

President Ronald Reagan once said, "Optimism is a choice and one of the most powerful ones you can make." It's fine to be objective, to have a good, clear, honest vision of what's happening around you. No matter what your experience, optimism always trumps pessimism. I think even "The Prince of Pessimism" would agree with that.

However, at the end of the day optimism must be balanced by realism. It's no good just hoping for the best. You've got to be willing to view life from all sides—no partisan bickering allowed. Take a good hard look and see things as they are, warts and all, and then do what you can to influence a positive outcome. President Reagan knew that. It's what gave him the courage to demand, "Mr. Gorbachev, tear down this wall." And the wall came down.

Chuck knew it too. Hope for the best, and try not to get caught up in all the hoopla.

CHUCKISM #42: WHATEVER!

Many of us love using this word to sum up our feelings when life doesn't make sense, and Chuck was no exception. It's a way of shaking our head at the world and moving beyond it. You hear it from your teenager just before she slams the bedroom door in your face, but for Chuck, "whatever" was not about "I don't care." It was about trust and surrender. Chuck was a master of moving on when the time was right.

Longtime NBA coach Mike Fratello told me, "When Chuck said, 'Whatever,' he meant, 'There's no need to talk any more.' There are no excuses, so don't just sit in your room and feel sorry for yourself. Focus on the important things and move on with your life. We all have to deal with tough stuff in our lives, so get over it."

Chuck's sense of humor was a key element in getting through life. Sports columnist Charlie Vincent observed, "Chuck never took himself too seriously. He loved being an NBA coach and loved wearing his Christian Dior warm-up suit. It had a 'CD' logo and Chuck got a big kick out of that."

Chuck simply didn't let life get him too lathered up. His "whatever" attitude helped him handle anything that came his way. He'd learned that your mindset, your worldview, your way of looking at the big picture, determines how you live. Armed with that wisdom, he kept on coaching to his last minute, as Dallas coach Rick Carlisle remembers well.

"In April of 2009, Chuck was in the last stages of his cancer battle, and I was in touch with him regularly," Rick told me. "Our Dallas team was battling for a playoff spot and had a big game at home with Phoenix. Chuck had remained my mentor and I called him before the game. He mustered up the energy to sound great over the phone, even though I knew he was suffering.

"Chuck would never suggest anything without me asking first, because he didn't want to impose. Finally he said to me, 'Wipe every-thing off the pregame board in the locker room. It's all about attitude.' The next day, I didn't write one word on the board. The answer seemed so simple. We won by about forty. It was a blow out."

Carlisle, by the way, now President of the NBA Coaches Association, designed a "CD" lapel pin that coaches and others wore during the 2009 playoffs as a tribute. Chuck loved it.

Longtime NBA center Danny Schayes observed, "Chuck Daly's famous 'whatever' really meant that none of the NBA stuff ever stuck to him. Come to work every day, do your job, stick to your own knitting, keep the unimportant stuff unimportant."

Attitude is everything. The late golfer Payne Stewart said, "A bad attitude is a bigger handicap than a bad swing." His contemporary Davis Love Jr. said, "Let your attitude determine your golf game. Don't let your golf game determine your attitude." There's not much in life you can control, but you have total control over your attitude. As Chuck might say, "Pick a good one."

CHUCKISM #43:
REBOUND. *REBOUND*. REBOUND!

Brendan Malone told me that frequently, when Chuck had his team in a huddle during a time out, he wouldn't say anything. Then when it came time to break, he would look in their eyes and simply say, "Rebound. *Rebound*. REBOUND." As a result, the players went back into the game with only one thing on their minds.

During the 2009 NBA championships, my daughter Karyn remembers the fun she had watching coaches Stan Van Gundy for the Magic and Phil Jackson with the Lakers on television. Their styles could not have been more opposite. A timeout would be called and Van Gundy had the guys in a huddle. The camera zoomed in on him, you could almost see the sweat beads and spit flying around the little ring, as Coach SVG exhorted his players to get out there and win. By contrast, Karyn said, over on the other side of the arena, the placid Phil Jackson circled his team—and said nothing. Not a word did he speak, until the very last moment. Then it was simply, "Move the ball. Make shots."

David Steele, longtime Orlando Magic broadcaster, told me, "In Chuck's first season with the Magic (1997-98), I had him lined up to tape a pre-game show. I was struggling with my equipment, which wasn't working properly. Chuck looked at me and said, 'Broadcasting 101.' His message was, 'Be prepared. Have a plan. No breakdowns.'"

Leaders, it's critical to be clear in communicating your goals. Be specific. Don't break from the huddle and leave your people wondering what to do next. That's how games are lost.

There's another way to look at this concept of the rebound—the bounce back we need when we're knocked down.

It involves having a strategy to win. That's what Chuck Daly brought to Detroit when he arrived in 1987. Veteran coach Dick Harter remembers the magical way Chuck got his key players to buy into his plan, one by one. After he sold center Bill Laimbeer he went after Isiah Thomas and won him over. The job was done. They took care of the rest. "At that point," Harter told me, "the Pistons were ready to move forward and become champions." The two key players were on board.

By the time he arrived in Orlando, Chuck had learned a thing or two about "buy in." When a player offered an idea for improving team play, Chuck would say, "It won't work." If the player believed strongly in his idea, he would knuckle down and try to prove Chuck wrong.

The secret to rebounding is pressing the reset button in your mind. Whatever it was that caused you to crash, reboot. Start over. Pick up the pieces and get back in the game. What happened yesterday doesn't matter anymore. It's where you're headed today that counts. That's how Chuck Daly saw it. I encourage you to adopt that attitude too.

CHUCKISM #44: HANDLE IT!

Back in the mid-1990s, I hired a young intern by the name of Annemarie Loflin. After her internship with me was up, Chuck Daly arrived as our coach and he needed an administrative assistant. Based on my high recommendation, Chuck hired Annemarie. She stayed on and worked for Doc Rivers after Chuck left in 1999, and when Doc became the Celtics head coach, she went with him to Boston. Like everyone who knew him, Annemarie has her own favorite "Chuckism" and this was it: *handle it.*

"He didn't want to know all the ins and outs of a task—he just wanted you to get it done. 'I'm leaving the details to you,' he would say."

That little observation can be summarized in one word: delegation. I believe it's the hardest thing for most executives to grasp. It sure was for me. Through much of my sports career I did everything and delegated nothing. Here's how I rationalized it: 1) I was better and smarter than everyone else, so why shouldn't I? Ha! 2) If I did a lot of delegating and the people I'd assigned did a really good job, wouldn't the owner think, *They're doing fine! What do we need Williams for? Why are we paying him the big bucks?* I couldn't run that risk, so I did it all.

In 1989 when the Magic started up, the NBA had grown so big I had no choice. I started delegating everything. It was one of the best discoveries I ever made.

That's my advice to you. Keep pushing opportunities down to your staff. In the process, they become a lot more energized and capable. Chuck understood we are really in the leadership development business, and that success without successors is not success at all. If we don't get the next generation of leaders ready to run with the baton in their hand, we're nothing but foam on the beach.

CHUCKISM #45: IT'S EASY TO SAY "YES" SIX MONTHS IN ADVANCE

One day, after Chuck had retired from coaching, we were talking on the phone about our speaking careers. Chuck said, "I accept these events way in advance, halfway thinking it will never get there. But then the time arrives. I've gotta get a speech ready, get packed up, go to the airport, fly to the event, schmooze with everybody at a party, give my talk, sign autographs, answer questions, be nice to everybody, then get up early the next morning to go through the airport and start the process all over again. It's easy to say 'yes' six months in advance."

Has that ever happened to you? People are clamoring to have you do this project or that event and, sincerely desiring to please, you say "yes." Then the day of the event arrives and you really don't want to go. You think, *Why did I ever accept that?* It's just not that important to you now.

Saying "no" may be one of the hardest things there is to do. We all want to please others and it's so easy to make them feel good by saying "yes" to their requests. But deep down, when crunch time comes, we don't want to do it.

So a good word to work on is "no." Here are a few suggestions on how to do it:

- "I really can't take on any more right now."

- "Thanks for the invitation, but I'm afraid I have to decline."

- "Thank you so much for thinking of me, but I'm afraid my calendar is overloaded and I have a commitment that day already."

Once Chuck got to the event, he was dazzling, of course, and people got to kibitz with the Olympic coach. But no one is going to condemn you if you say "no."

John Nash, the former general manager of four NBA franchises, was director of the Big 5 college program in Philadelphia when Chuck was coaching at the University of Pennsylvania. Every year before the season starts, the Big 5 holds a coaches' luncheon for the media where the different coaches all speak. John told me, "For back-to-back seasons, Chuck gave the same talk. The theme was, 'You're Either in the Box or You're Out of the Box.' His message was about commitment. You're either committed to the team [organization, business, ministry, or project] or you're not."

That was another "Chuckism"—"You're either in the box or you're out of the box." So many people try to put a foot in both worlds. They want to be married but also want to be single. They want the team to do well but are concerned with individual statistics. They want a college degree and a party life too. We really can't live that way with any measure of success. Life revolves around commitment—to a mate, to an employer, to a president, to a coach, to a university, or to "whatever."

The companion word to commitment is *loyalty*. That's a lost art in our time, but an important quality. We need to rediscover it. I see it in my family. Four of our children are brothers we adopted from the Philippines. They're all adults now in their late twenties and early thirties, and a true band of brothers. If one starts drowning, they do everything they can to lift him up. Old enough to remember their lives before adoption, they've never forgotten their roots. They've never forgotten the loyalty that always moved the older brothers to help the younger ones.

You may be thinking that the world isn't showing you much loyalty, so why should you give back? That's a dangerous road to get stuck on. Be the best person you can be and let the world sort out the rest.

Learn to say "no" in order to say "yes" to what really matters. That's what Chuck Daly would tell you.

CHUCKISM #46:
IGNORE

Duke basketball coach Mike Krzyzewski remembers Chuck Daly well. "During preparation for the 1992 Olympics," Mike recalls, "the two college coaches on Chuck's staff were P. J. [Carlesimo] and me. During meetings, we were always writing everything down. Chuck eventually said to us, 'You are both writing everything down and taking notes all the time. You need to understand one word: *Ignore*.'

"Most of the things you see will eventually work out if you ignore them and see what happens," Coach K observes. "In other words, don't make something small into something big. Small problems tend to stay small problems or go away if they're ignored. Chuck was the best at putting those kinds of things into proper perspective. He was a true ambassador for the game of basketball."

This "Chuckism" gives me pause to grin over my old friend's sage wisdom. How many of our problems—you know, those mountains that obsess our lives for hours, maybe even days—turn out to be nothing much after all? Things really do have a way of working out.

That's not to contradict his earlier "everything happens to me" message, but simply to state that, while our hoped-for plans may never see the light of day, life itself has a way of shaking things out if we are patient. We should take time to be prepared. But there's really no need to micromanage every moment of every day. This advice goes hand-in-hand with the "Chuckism" that says, *It is what it is*. Don't sweat the little things. You and all those around you will be much happier if you take that attitude.

CHUCKISM #47:
NOT A PROBLEM!

Here's an expression that's become almost a by-word these days—and usually in the world of customer service. "Not a problem!" the salesperson often says. If placing your order were a problem, why would the business exist in the first place? "Not a problem" is not always logically used, but when Chuck Daly said it—there was meaning. And the meaning was deep and rich.

Chuck had seen plenty of problems in his life. A child of the Great Depression, he understood scrimping and doing without. As a high school basketball coach, he knew what it was to have his personal dreams put on hold—until that magical day Vic Bubas called and offered him an assistant's position at Duke. And as a young man growing up in a turbulent period in American history, Chuck witnessed a lot of the problems people caused for each other.

Wayne Embry had retired after playing eleven seasons with the Cincinnati Royals, the Boston Celtics, and the Milwaukee Bucks. "In 1971," he told me, "I took a job with the Boston Parks and Recreation Department. You had to live within the city limits, so we moved into the Jamaica Plains section of town. We were unpacking in our new home when, out the window, we saw our next-door neighbor building a fence in the pouring rain. Pretty soon there was a knock on the door. It was Chuck Daly welcoming us to the neighborhood. Turned out he lived three doors down. 'Your neighbor here has tried to rally the neighborhood to keep you out,' he said. 'I've challenged him and I'm ready to take him on.' That was my introduction to Chuck."

Issues that troubled others deeply—like the prejudices that still boiled over in many parts of the country at that time—were "not a problem" for Chuck Daly. That statement Chuck made to Wayne Embry is the reason these inter-personal conflicts were "not a problem" for him. Chuck had a firm grasp on the difference between right and wrong. He knew where lines needed to be drawn and where they needed to be erased.

Chuck often told the story of the day he was teaching a philosophy class to some athletes at Duke. He would say, "I'm telling everyone, 'you can get on the players—that's OK. Because once you leave the court it's all over. It's forgotten.'

"This football player gets right up and says, 'That's not right. It's not forgotten. Whatever you say is remembered. You can't get on a player one minute and expect him to forget it in the next minute.' The guy caught me by surprise, but that statement—what he had to say that day—has meant as much to me as anything I've ever heard in my life. I learned more in those few moments that at any other time in my life."

During a teaching moment, it was the teacher who learned the lesson. Because Chuck was humble and open to those moments, he rose above the tense times many of us consider problems in our lives.

Is there a situation in your life that's gone on longer than it should have? Could the line separating you from another be erased by a simple, "I'm sorry"? Learn this Chuck Daly lesson and you, too, can say, "Not a problem."

CHAPTER 8: WHATEVER YOU DO, DO IT WITH STYLE

CHUCKISM #48: WHAT ARE YOU DOING?

Broadcaster Jim Gray was Chuck's close friend and has an endless supply of stories about traveling together and hearing Chuck ask this startling question. "If I turned a street too soon," Jim recalls, "Chuck would say, 'What are you *doing*?' At a restaurant, if I ordered incorrectly, it was, 'What are you *doing*?' It's the kind of question that definitely gets your attention."

One weekend when Chuck was head coach of the Magic, we were all flying to New York for the NBA All-Star Weekend. My wife, Ruth, came along, too, to enjoy time with me at all the gala events. As usual, I had piles of books with me and read the entire weekend, including during the game. I didn't realize Chuck was watching, but in retrospect I'm glad he was. At an opportune moment, he pulled me aside.

"What are you *doing*?" Chuck said. "Do you realize you haven't spoken a word to your wife this entire trip? All you've done is read those books. You'd better watch it!" When I told Ruth what he said, her response was, "Thank goodness for Chuck Daly!"

Is there a Chuck Daly in your life? It could be your best friend, your life mate, your spiritual partner, your mom or dad, or a mentor—but we all need someone who'll whip our heads around at just the right moment with that question: What are you *doing*?

So pay attention! Chuck's question might just be the wake-up call you need to get your life in order.

CHUCKISM #49: ALL OF YOU WANT TO BE IN MY SEAT—BUT IT'S HOT UP HERE!

Leaders must think like leaders. Chuck Daly practiced this principle from his youngest days. Take the focus off yourself and realize you've got a team depending on you—for strategy, inspiration, encouragement, and direction.

Former Magic player Jeff Turner was working as a color analyst for the Orlando Magic when Chuck Daly served as our coach—the fourth coach in franchise history—back in 1997. Here's his story:

"I had retired two seasons prior as a player and had joined the club's radio broadcast team. My position put me at every practice, on the team plane, and courtside to watch one of the most fascinating men I have ever watched work an NBA sideline. When I think about Chuck Daly, I am not reminded of Xs and Os, or great victories or losses, but more about the way he related to his staff and those of us on the periphery of the Magic traveling party. There was never a doubt about who was in charge, yet Chuck had a unique and, in my opinion, humorous way of communicating with and empowering his staff to be the best.

"One of my favorite memories is of a game that was not going well for the Magic. The team was in the middle of a lengthy road trip and clearly not playing with a lot of energy or focus. Coach Daly had used several timeouts to get them going and he was up and prowling the sidelines more than usual. He made several adjustments offensively and defensively, changed line-ups out on the floor, but nothing was working. After one possession in which the clock expired before the Magic could get off a shot, Daly turned to his coaching staff and said, 'OK, all of you geniuses. Give me something! All of you want to sit in my seat—but it's hot up here!'

"Several years later I left broadcasting for a new challenge. I accepted a position as an administrator in charge of leadership development and head boy's basketball coach at Lake Highland Preparatory School in Orlando. In my first game as head coach, I found myself thinking about that game and what Chuck had said. Twenty-five years of playing basketball, learning from some great coaches, and the knowledge that comes with experience as a player had not prepared me for sitting in the 'hot seat,' as Chuck referred to it. Twelve young men were looking at me for quick decisions, inspiring words to lift them up after a mistake, or that special play that would give them confidence for that much needed basket. I was like an assistant coach focusing on individual players and plays and not seeing the big picture my job called for.

"Chuck understood that his assistants needed to start thinking like head coaches. He had challenged them that night in his own special way to think bigger and begin preparing for the day when they would be leading their own teams.

"I'm sure he had no idea that a former player turned broadcaster—whom he referred to as 'left hander'—was listening. I count myself as one of the lucky ones who had the chance to watch and learn from a great teacher. Thanks, Chuck. It's still hot in the chair, but I can deal with the heat a little easier—thanks to you."

It takes boldness and courage to be a great leader. Jeff Turner's story should inspire us all.

CHUCKISM #50:
SEDUCED BY THE COMPETITION

In the spring of 1997, the Magic had a coaching need. And Chuck Daly had a competition need. Chuck had retired from coaching. He'd had his run with Detroit, with the Nets, and he was done, peacefully living the retired life—until the Magic lured him out from hiding. We held a big press conference to introduce him as our new head coach. "What made you decide to return to these NBA wars?" the press wanted to know . . . to which Chuck replied with one eloquent phrase, "The seduction of the competition."

The more I've thought about that statement over the years, the more I think it's what drives all great athletes and coaches. Yes, the money is fine, the notoriety is fine, the fame is all well and good. But at the end of day, they have a compulsive need to compete—to put my skills up against yours, my team against yours. That's what is on the mind of a coach.

After a few years away from the excitement, Chuck was not fulfilled. The Magic's offer was just the right bait to pull him back into the all-consuming world of professional basketball. Chuck needed to compete. He often said, "I'm just a lifer, and proud of it." Once he'd trained his focus on basketball as his life's work, there was no looking back. So naturally, he couldn't stay away.

After two seasons with the Magic, he retired again—until the day Memphis Grizzlies owner Michael Heisley called. "When I first bought the team, I hired Chuck as an adviser," Heisley recalls, "I considered him a gift from God. We spent hours talking about coaching philosophy." Natural born competitors recognize one another.

Chuck had spent his whole life seduced by the competition. He'd been a broadcaster and enjoyed it. But when the game ended, he'd go back to his room, not caring who won or lost. He'd taken time to prepare, of course, but there was no knot in the stomach over what was coming. Chuck missed the intensity of the daily competition.

This is true of all of us. We live in an enormously competitive society. Whether we're competing for college, for a job, for a promotion, for the hand of a girlfriend, or competing to win an election, everything in our country is based on competition. Don't shy from it. Don't run from it. It can be intimidating, especially in the business world, but my counsel is to welcome your competition. Like iron sharpening iron, it's what gives us our edge and makes us the best we can be. It pulls out qualities we'd have missed if not for the challenge. We are at our sharpest when we're competing intensely.

There was another aspect of competition that intrigued Chuck—the ever-present subplot. He'd say, "There's always a game within the game." You might have two players who'd competed since high school, or a referee with a chip on his shoulder over one player in the game. It's a constant current running under the surface of every competition. There is always a game within the game.

It's true anywhere you have people—businesses, churches, non-profit groups, institutions, schools, major corporations. There's always a subplot weaving itself through the bigger tapestry. Chuck was keenly aware of that.

So keep paying attention. Keep your eyes and ears open and alert to all threads in every situation. Then you'll be ready when the competition comes to town.

CHUCKISM #51:
CHUCKDALY

He was born Charles Jerome Daly on July 20, 1930. But I have a feeling only his mother called him Charles, and no one I heard ever used Jerome. Many of us who knew and loved him simply called him "CD." His penchant for fine clothes led former Piston forward John Salley to nickname him, "Daddy Rich." Other monikers included "The Prince of Pessimism," "Hall of Famer," or simply "Coach." Though he never played professionally, he was "named" in 1996 one of the ten top coaches in NBA history, with a 638-437 record over fourteen seasons. But one day his brother, Bud, reminded me that when he answered the phone or recorded his voicemail message, it was always: "Chuckdaly." We had a good laugh remembering how Chuck said it—so rapid fire, it was like one word. Chuckdaly. The name became his brand.

If you were a product named Chuckdaly, what would you look like? I hope by now, through the stories we've told in this book, you have a pretty good picture in your mind. But just in case the image is still a little fuzzy, let me offer a little more clarification.

Sportscaster Bernie Smilovitz saw him this way: "Chuck Daly loved being Chuck Daly. He felt more comfortable as he kept moving up the ladder of success. Really, he was every man's man."

To Dick Harter, Chuck's assistant coach in Detroit, he was, "the only coach ever who liked every player he ever coached. He kept things positive and was never sarcastic. The man had no bad qualities."

Gina Coleman, wife of former Nets player Derrick Coleman, worked in the Nets front office when Chuck was there. She remembers, "Chuck was a warm sweet loving guy, always smiling. He went out of his way to treat staff well. Chuck was a true father figure to Derrick."

Duke's Mike Krzyzewski was an assistant to Chuck on the Olympic team. He told ESPN, "There was no better ambassador for the game of basketball than Chuck Daly" ("Daly Led Pistons to Pair of Titles," May 10, 2009; http://sports.espn.go.com/nba/news/story?id=4153982).

New York Daily News sportswriter Dick Weiss saw in Chuck "a great college recruiter. He could sell any kid he wanted and loved doing it. Then he could coach them just as well. But with it all, Chuck was always so self-deprecating."

The "Chuckdaly" brand meant the finest in quality and customer satisfaction—whether we're talking clothes, coaching, or community. He always put out the highest effort and always put others first—and he did this his whole life long. As a result, there are young people out there right now living out their success stories because of Chuck Daly—people like Shayain Gustavsp.

A student and manager for the men's basketball team at Northwood University in West Palm Beach back in 2007, Shayain impressed Chuck with her stage presence as a speaker at a local Outstanding Business Leaders awards dinner. Chuck, one of the evening's honorees, was a familiar face at Northwood games. He called Shayain over to his table and asked if she'd like help finding a job after graduation.

"Obviously, my response was 'Yes!'" Shayain recalled. "Mr. Daly pulled out his phone and said, 'I have a friend by the name of Pat Williams. He will help you out. Here is his number.' As I scrambled for paper and a pen, Mr. Daly said, 'Make sure you tell him you know me, and he will do something for you. He's a great guy.'

"So I called, and the first thing Mr. Williams said to me was, 'Get your Master's degree. The sports industry is very competitive and you'll need your Masters.' He named four schools and I chose the DeVos Sports Business Management Program at the University of Central Florida. I have a semester left to graduate and then I'm on my way to getting a PhD in Sports Administration. It's all thanks to Mr. Daly for giving me the right guidance and being the great man that he was. I wouldn't be here if it wasn't for him. I will miss you, Coach, dearly." Shayain sums it up well for all of us who knew Chuck.

A product named "Chuckdaly" would be known for its trailblazing acumen. Cleveland Cavaliers coach Mike Brown told NBA.com that Chuck was, to coaches, what fellows like Wilt Chamberlain, Michael Jordan, and Dr. J were for the players. "He's paved the way," Brown said. "He's allowed us to make the salaries we make. He's allowed us to, in people's eyes, be held in a high regard in terms of the level of where we're coaching. Without pioneers like him, guys that paved the way for guys like us, we wouldn't be enjoying the fruits of their labor like we are right now" (http://www.nba.com/2009/news/features/05/09/daly. obit.peterson/index.html).

Even rival coaches were touched by the Daly magic. "In the heat of those battles," Lakers coach Phil Jackson told ESPN, "Chuck was always a friend of coaches. A good guy. He was always in the coaching fraternity and always extended a friendly hand" ("Daly Led Pistons to Pair of Titles," May 10, 2009; http://sports.espn.go.com/nba/news/story?id=4153982).

NBA Commissioner David Stern, in his official remarks following Coach Daly's death, said, "Chuck did much more than coach basketball games. He positively impacted everyone he met, both personally and professionally, and his love of people and the game of basketball helped develop the next generation of coaches" (http://www.nba.com/2009/news/05/09/stern.daly/index.html).

If you were a product named "Chuckdaly," your simplest words and gestures would become lifetime memories. Doug Collins, who worked with Chuck in the 76ers organization, remembers the time in July of 2008 when Coach Mike Krzyzewski invited him to come speak in Las Vegas to the U.S. Olympic team about his experience playing at the 1972 games in Munich. "My speech went very well and everyone seemed pleased," Collins told me. "That night at the banquet I walked by the table where Chuck was sitting. He said, 'Doug, I heard you did a great job today. I'm proud of you.' That was the last time I saw Chuck, but those words meant the world to me."

Could Chuck have known those would be his last words to Doug Collins? Could Doug have known? Remember the enduring, positive power of your influence.

After Chuck's death, Dream Team player and basketball legend Michael Jordan said, "My only regret is that I did not play for Chuck as my real coach." When Brendan Suhr heard that remark, he commented, "That statement by Michael says a ton about Chuck." That's the way a product named "Chuckdaly" would be remembered—as something people who missed it wished they hadn't.

Finally, if you were a product named "Chuckdaly," you would keep giving with everything you have as long as you possibly could. Veteran Dick Stockton had this to say about his last visit with Chuck in March of 2009: "He was battling cancer with all he had. The NCAA tournament was going on and March Madness was raging. There was Chuck, watching the Pistons and the Nets in just another NBA game. With sixty days left to live, Chuck was coaching both of those teams as if they were his own."

On Wednesday, May 13, 2009, hundreds gathered to pay final respects to Chuck. The Detroit Pistons sent their entire front office to his funeral service and his team of "Bad Boys,"—including Isiah Thomas, Joe Dumars, Vinnie Johnson, Rick Mahorn and Bill Laimbeer—served as pallbearers.

Thomas said of his longtime coach, "Chuck was a fighter, and he fought until his dying breath. But right up to the end, he was more concerned about everyone else, all his basketball friends, making sure they were all right with this. That's the kind of guy he was. I think this turnout speaks for itself" (http://www.nba.com/2009/news/features/05/13/daly.funeral/index.html).

An Associated Press article on Chuck's funeral reported that Dallas coach Rick Carlisle left for Denver right after the service to lead his team in a game. "Missing this [funeral] was not an option," he said.

Referring to Miami Heat coach Pat Riley, the article concluded, "As he walked away from the church, Riley pulled on a pair of sunglasses to mask his tears. 'I think we all aspired to be like him,' he said, softly. 'We couldn't'" (http://sports.espn.go.com/nba/news/story?id=4164565).

Because of the singular life he led, because he was a man of extraordinary character and class, the brand "Chuckdaly" will live on well beyond the man's life span. It's my hope that, after reading this book, it will live on in you. Give your best every day. Change lives with your words. Keep pressing on. Squeeze every drop out of your life. There is no greater "Daly Wisdom" than that.

Pat's Final Thoughts

Chuckism #52:
We Want to Be Happy After the Games

Rollie Massimino worked hard for Chuck back at the University of Pennsylvania and did a lot of recruiting. It was Chuck who gave Rollie his start in the big time world of college basketball.

Rollie went on to become the head coach at Villanova University, where he led them to an NCAA title in 1985. He was one of the most visible, high-level college coaches of that era. Later he coached at the University of Nevada at Las Vegas and Cleveland State, and then retired to south Florida.

But the game kept wooing him back—"seduced by the competition," as Chuck might say. Before long, Rollie, now in his seventies, became the head coach at this little school in West Palm Beach, Northwood University. Many of his friends lived there—Billy Cunningham, the Hall of Famer, Bill Raftery, John Havlicek, and Bobby Orr, the former hockey great, and of course, Chuck Daly. They all became great Northwood fans and would go to games together. It's a story with definite movie potential.

From the beginning of his career, Rollie had been Chuck's protégé. So in 2009, as the cancer was consuming Chuck's life, Rollie began making daily visits to see him in the hospital. He was still Rollie's coach.

One day, Chuck said to him, "Rollie, did you make any calls?" It was the kind of question he'd have asked back in their days at Penn, when the young assistant coach would be out on the recruiting trail.

Chuck is talking to Rollie, who is now a coaching legend himself, and saying, "Did you make any calls, Rollie? Did you get any players today? We want to be happy after the games."

The essence of Chuck Daly's life was, "We want to be happy after the games." And there's only one thing that makes us happy: winning. Wins make us happy. Losses leave us very unhappy.

Chuck, ever the coach, ever the mentor, right to his last breath, is reminding Rollie—"Rollie, you'd better get out of here. You'd better go sign some players. Because all of your famous friends are going to be a lot happier over their lobster dinners after a win."

Life is all about wins and losses. Aren't we a lot happier when we have a successful bottom line in our business? Aren't we a lot happier when our military wins a war? Aren't we a lot happier when our university has graduated a crop of outstanding students? Aren't we a lot happier when our church's roll call is increasing and the building program is ahead of schedule? Chuck had a very clear perspective on life and on his profession: you play to win. Right to your last breath.

I remember years ago, at the Orlando Magic Youth Foundation Banquet, we honored General Norman Schwarzkopf. I was assigned as his tagalong during the reception. At one point, I said to him, "General

Schwarzkopf, do you ever look at your life in disbelief? After all, here you were a longtime military officer and suddenly this mad man goes crazy over in Iraq and invades Kuwait, we're thrown into a war that you head up, and you end up as this highly revered military leader. Now you're writing books and making speeches, you're in demand, and people are absolutely agog over you. Does that ever just blow your mind?" And General Schwarzkopf said to me, "Well, nobody would remember me if we hadn't won." We all like winners.

Chuck Daly was a winner—in basketball and in life. I learned a lot of lessons from him over the years and I've shared them as a tribute to our friend.

Take all of these Chuckisms, apply them to your life on a daily basis. Keep grinding. Battle through the tough times. Fight through discouragement. Never stop learning. Don't get carried away with yourself when you're on top of the world. Don't give up when you're at the bottom of the well. Keep your eyes intensely focused on one thing: win the game. Win in the game of life. Keep pursuing victory. We want to be happy after the games!

Thanks, Chuck, for showing us the way.

We'll never forget you.

Grateful thanks to those who contributed stories
and memories for this book:

Mike Abdenour

Mitch Albom

Nick Anderson

Harvey Araton

Darrell Armstrong

Tony Barone, Sr.

Larry Bird

George Blaha

Fran Blinebury

Kim Bohuny

Hubie Brown

P.J. Brown

Vic Bubas

Bill Campbell

Ron Campbell

Ray Carazo

P.J. Carlesimo

Rick Carlisle

Don Casey

Derrick Coleman

Gina Coleman

Doug Collins

Kathy Collins

Lonnie Cooper

Scott Crites

Billy Cunningham

Cydney Daly

Adrian Dantley

Matt Dobek

Michael Doleac

Andy Dolich

Joe Dumars

Wayne Embry	Bobby Jones
Nancy Emery	Mike Krzyzewski
Julius Erving	Bill Laimbeer
Patrick Ewing	Jerry Lewis
Mike Fratello	Annemarie Loflin
Neil Funk	Jimmy Lynum
John Gabriel	Bill Lyon
Howard Garfinkel	Don Magnuson
John Ginopolis	Rick Mahorn
Jim Gray	Brendan Malone
Matt Guokas	Alex Martins
Shayain Gustavsp	Rollie Massimino
Matt Harpring	Jack McCloskey
Dick Harter	Brian McIntyre
Dan Hauser	Eric Musselman
Michael Heisley	John Nash
Sonny Hill	Gary Nicholas
Harry Hutt	Bo Outlaw
Phil Jasner	Dr. Ben Paolucci

Rodney Powell

Bill Raftery

Jack Ramsay

Ronnie Rothstein

Bob Ryan

Danny Schayes

Wendy Schayes

Jack Scheuer

Fred Shabel

Don Shane

Paul Silas

Bernie Smilovitz

Jim Spanarkel

Bob Staak

David Steele

Ed Stefanski

Tom Sterner

Dick Stockton

Brendan Suhr

Rod Thorn

Kelly Tripucka

Jeff Turner

Bob Vander Weide

Dick Versace

Charlie Vincent

Tim Walsh

Bucky Waters

Bob Weinhauer

Dick Weiss

Lenny Wilkens

Evan "Big Cat" Williams

Tom Wilson

Adam Witty

Bob Zuffelato

ACKNOWLEDGMENTS

With deep appreciation I acknowledge the support and guidance of the following people who helped make this book possible:

Special thanks to Rich DeVos, Bob Vander Weide, and Alex Martins of the Orlando Magic.

I have been highly honored to have reconnected with so many people who, like myself, knew and loved Chuck Daly. I am grateful to you all for sharing your stories with me for this book.

Thanks also to my writing partner, Peggy Matthews Rose, for her superb contributions in shaping this manuscript.

Hats off to four dependable associates—my assistant Latria Leak, my trusted and valuable colleague Andrew Herdliska, my ace typist, Fran Thomas, and my longtime adviser, Ken Hussar.

Hearty thanks also go to my friend Adam Witty and his capable staff at Advantage Media Group. Thank you all for believing that we had something important to share and for providing the support and the forum to say it.

And finally, special thanks and appreciation go to my wonderful and supportive family. They are truly the backbone of my life.

—Pat Williams

You can contact Pat Williams at:

Pat Williams

c/o Orlando Magic

8701 Maitland Summit Boulevard

Orlando, FL 32810

(407) 916-2404

pwilliams@orlandomagic.com

Visit Pat Williams' website at: www.PatWilliamsMotivate.com

If you would like to set up a speaking engagement for Pat Williams, please call or Andrew Herdliska at 407-916-2401 or e-mail him at aherdliska@orlandomagic.com.

We would love to hear from you. Please send your comments about this book to Pat Williams at the above address or in care of our publisher at the address below. Thank you.

Adam Witty

Advantage Media Group

P.O. Box 272

Charleston, South Carolina 29402

www.amglive.com

Tree Neutral™

Advantage Media Group is proud to be a part of the Tree Neutral™ program. Tree Neutral offsets the number of trees consumed in the production and printing of this book by taking proactive steps such as planting trees in direct proportion to the number of trees used to print books. To learn more about Tree Neutral, please visit **www.treeneutral.com.** To learn more about Advantage Media Group's commitment to being a responsible steward of the environment, please visit **www.advantagefamily.com/green**

Daly Wisdom is available in bulk quantities at special discounts for corporate, institutional, and educational purposes. To learn more about the special programs Advantage Media Group offers, please visit **www.KaizenUniversity.com** or call 1.866.775.1696.

Advantage Media Group is a leading publisher of business, motivation, and self-help authors. Do you have a manuscript or book idea that you would like to have considered for publication? Please visit **www.amgbook.com**